*Special services
of rural workers' organisations*

Special services
of rural workers' organisations

A workers' education manual

International Labour Office   Geneva

ISBN 92-2-101813-X

First published 1978

Printed by Imprimeries Populaires Arts graphiques, Geneva, Switzerland

The majority of the world's poor are rural workers, whether they be wage earners, self-employed subsistence owner-occupiers or landless labourers. It is now becoming increasingly recognised that the improvement of the conditions of life and work of these millions of workers is in large measure dependent upon the extent to which they can be mobilised—both to help themselves and to contribute to national development.

This was one of the reasons underlying the adoption by the International Labour Conference in June 1975 of a Convention and a Recommendation concerning Organisations of Rural Workers and Their Role in Economic and Social Development. These instruments defined the term "rural workers", affirmed the right of them all (both employed and self-employed) to freedom of association, set out the conditions necessary for the development of their organisations, outlined the roles that they might undertake and suggested ways and means by which their development might be furthered.

However, there is a world of difference between agreeing that certain aims are desirable and actually achieving those aims. This book is intended to help towards bridging that gap in so far as rural workers' organisations are concerned.

The aim of a workers' organisation is to provide a service or services to its members. Unless it does provide such a service or services, along lines determined by its members, its days will be numbered. The first and traditional service of a wage earners' union is that of bargaining over the wages and conditions of its members. In a developing country an organisation of rural workers will seldom be able to raise wage levels sufficiently to enable its members to meet their many pressing needs; in order to satisfy some of these needs, the organisation has to find ways and means of providing its members with a different kind of service—in other words, a "special service".

The traditional major service of an organisation of self-employed rural workers (sharecroppers, tenant farmers, small owner-occupiers and landless labourers)—which, of course, is by its very nature not concerned with negotiating wages—is that of pressure-group activities to achieve the reforms necessary to improve the lot of its members. But reforms do not come quickly, and in the meantime the members have many urgent needs for which the organisation may be able to provide a special service.

This book looks into these special services: their nature, their development, their problems, their advantages, their pitfalls. It is intended both to assist rural workers' organisations to extend the services they already provide, and to lead workers' educators and others who wish to help in the development of rural organisations towards a better understanding of the ways in which they could do so. The presentation—the original text of which was prepared for the ILO by Mr. Edward M. Colbert, a lifelong trade unionist with many years of practical experience with rural workers' organisations in developing countries—is based on actual cases of special services in the rural sector. It is not a textbook: it is a practical guide illustrating and explaining what can be done in a field which is important both for the rural workers themselves and for the countries in which they live.

Contents

Photographs

The International Labour Office wishes to make acknowledgement to the Food
and Agriculture Organisation of the United Nations, Rome, for permission to
reproduce the lower photograph on p. 48. All the other photographs are taken
from the ILO Photo Library, Geneva.

Introduction

Rural workers and their organisations

In developing countries workers' organisations are not always able to further and defend all the interests of their members by the traditional methods of negotiation and representation. Under such circumstances many workers' organisations have introduced special services as a means of trying to satisfy some of the outstanding needs of their members. This has been particularly true as far as rural workers' organisations are concerned.

A "rural worker" is any person engaged in agriculture or a related occupation in a rural area, whether as a wage earner or as a self-employed person.[1]

Wage earners in the rural sector include all permanent, seasonal and temporary or casual workers employed for wages in agriculture and related occupations: many of these, especially those whose employment is temporary or seasonal, may also be migrant workers.

The self-employed group includes such persons as sharecroppers, tenants, small owner-occupiers, squatters and nomads. Tenants, share-croppers and similar categories of agricultural worker pay a landlord for the use of the land. The payment may take the form of a fixed rent in cash, in kind, in labour or in a combination of these; or it may be a rent in kind consisting of an agreed share of the produce; or the tenant or sharecropper may be remunerated by a share of the produce.

Small owner-occupiers are cultivators of individually held or communally held land who derive their main income from agriculture, by working the land either themselves or with the help only of their families or of occasional outside labour. On the other hand, those who permanently employ workers or employ a substantial number of seasonal workers or have any land cultivated by sharecroppers or tenants are not themselves considered to be rural workers.

---

[1] The full internationally agreed definition of a rural worker is set out in the ILO Rural Workers' Organisations Convention, 1975 (No. 141), see the appendix to this book.

Landless labourers are those who live in rural areas and who have no access to land to cultivate (through either ownership, tenancy or common usage) and who therefore depend for their livelihood on hiring out their labour for wages. In practice, the term may also be considered to include those who have access only to a plot of land that is too small to support them and their family. The rural unemployed—those who would be independent cultivators if they could find land to work, or who would be wage earners if they could find employment—may also be looked upon as landless labourers.

Special mention must be made of "family workers", generally the wife and children of the rural worker, who often work beside him, or in his place where there is an extensive migration of male workers seeking employment, or where the accepted tradition is that the woman supervises the cultivation of the small farm plot while the husband works elsewhere. In some countries there are many rural women workers, especially in the self-employed and casually employed groups.

These categories of rural worker often overlap. The same worker may belong to two or more categories at the same time or over the course of the year. For example, a rural worker may own a small plot of land or be a sharecropper on a small plot and also work as a wage earner on a seasonal or casual basis.

Traditional trade union services

A rural workers' organisation, like an urban or industrial workers' organisation, is formed by the coming together of workers in an association which is on a continuing and democratic basis, dependent on its own resources and independent of patronage, the purpose of which is to further and defend the interests of the members. Workers' unions traditionally undertake this task in many ways. Through collective bargaining with employers they obtain for their members the most favourable terms with respect to wages, hours, conditions of work and (depending on the needs of the members and the strength of the union) many other interests of the members. Through pressure-group activities, they make representations on behalf of their members to government, to political parties and to society as a whole, with a view to influencing decisions relating to national and local policies, legislation and administration affecting the interests of members. They provide legal services to members with respect to any work-related interests to be furthered or defended. They provide information and education services which keep members informed and advised of their rights as workers and as citizens, of their rights under the collective agreement negotiated by the union and under the laws of their country, of their union's activities in seeking changes in the agreement and changes in national policies and legislation, and of events and circumstances which may further or threaten members' interests.

Unions of rural wage earners exactly parallel their urban and industrial counterparts as regards the traditional methods used to further and defend these interests.[1] Peasant unions [2] (organisations of self-employed rural workers) employ most of the methods used by unions of wage earners. They provide their members with legal services and with information and education services. Peasant unions normally go much further than unions of wage earners in providing representation on behalf of their members, because all the peasant's interests require furthering and defending within the economic, political and social life of his country. Representation by pressure-group activities is often the principal reason for a peasant union's existence, and—particularly in developing countries—the peasant is frequently demanding reforms of the society in which he lives, and seeking a restructuring of the economic, social and political life of the rural sector.[3]

Special services

Perhaps the simplest way of explaining what is meant by the term "special services" is to say that the term includes *any activity by a union to meet any members' needs which are not being met by the traditional union methods* of negotiation, pressure-group activities or representation.

Rural workers' organisations in developing countries (or developing regions within developed countries) very often find themselves in this position: there are pressing needs of members which cannot be immedi-

---

[1] For a detailed treatment of the nature and activities of rural workers' organisations, both those for wage earners and those for the self-employed, see ILO: *Structure and functions of rural workers' organisations* (Geneva, 1978).

[2] In the literature dealing with rural workers the term "peasant" is applied to the self-employed rural worker, such as the sharecropper, tenant or small owner-occupier.

[3] The exact reforms being sought by peasant unions in developing countries vary with the particular situation in which the peasants find themselves in their own country. Generally, however, they include land reform and agrarian reform. Land reform includes reform of the land tenure system and/or the abolition of landlordism with redistribution of the land. Reform of the land tenure system includes, inter alia, the regulation or prohibition of crop sharing; security of tenure; limitation on rent charges; and payment for improvements made by the tenant. Redistribution of the land is generally thought of as implying "land to the tiller" and includes land consolidation whereby the tiller can become the owner of a "family size" farm. Land belonging to the State can also be redistributed. Agrarian reform or integrated agrarian reform includes land reform and implies that the mere transfer of land to those who till the soil is not sufficient reform and is meaningless if the necessary credit, technical assistance, markets and transport facilities are not provided to increase production and the amount received by the peasants for their production. Peasant unions add a third element to their definition of agrarian reform: the participation of the representatives of the peasants in the reform is itself a *part* of the reform and indeed, the basic step in that reform.

ately satisfied by negotiations or representation; the lack of economic development or peculiar political or legal restraints in the country or area in which the union exists may preclude furthering and defending some interests of the members in the traditional ways. The union therefore establishes some type of project or scheme by which it tries to service these outstanding needs. If the need can be satisfied by traditional methods, the union does not need to become involved in special services.

This way of defining special services emphasises an important aspect of the term that needs to be kept in mind; special services are only used to meet those needs of members which cannot at the present time be met in any other way. Special services are only a means; they are not an end. The end for a workers' organisation is always, and simply, to further and defend the interests of its members.

Another way of explaining what is meant by special services is by looking at instances where the needs of members have been met by such services.

For example, in developed countries, rural workers' organisations are often able to further the interests of members and their families with respect to education by the traditional method of representation to government, in order to obtain the establishment and operation of the necessary educational facilities in the rural sector. In developing countries, a government may not have the resources to do this, or may put a low priority on rural schooling. Some rural wage earners' organisations in this situation are able to negotiate with the employer that the latter should establish and operate primary schools for the first few years of the education of members' children. Other unions, however, are obliged to develop projects or schemes of their own, either alone or in conjunction with others. Such a case, when a union directly establishes such a project or scheme, is an example of a "special service" (in the sense in which the term is used in this book) provided to meet an outstanding need of members.

Another illustration is that of a workers' organisation whose members do not have access to a savings and loan service—a credit union. The union consequently establishes a credit union—and provides a special service to meet a need that could not be obtained by negotiation or representation. This example could be applicable in both developed and developing countries.

Another illustration, based on the needs or interests of peasants, is a scheme or project for the marketing of the produce of peasant members. In developed countries, peasant organisations are often able to obtain marketing facilities and related improvements for members by representation to government. In developing countries, peasant unions often try to develop union-operated marketing activities for members when they are unable to obtain them by the traditional method.

Case studies

In an attempt to make this book as useful as possible, the "case study" method is employed. Existing or planned examples of special services provided by rural workers' organisations are presented, though with a few adaptations here and there to fit the requirements of a book designed to give as much information as possible on the efforts, problems, successes, failures and experiences of rural workers' organisations in relation to special services. As is the custom and one of the values of the case study method, the organisations are not identified. This allows analysis of the negative as well as the positive aspects of the experiences.

In Part I five case studies are presented, in which all the special services developed by each of five different organisations are examined. Case A presents the many special services designed by a strong, long-established national union to meet some of the needs of its wage earner members. Case B examines the special services developed and operated by a 30-year-old national peasant federation functioning in a situation where significant agrarian reform has taken place. Case C deals with the many special services of a new, local organisation of sharecroppers, tenant farmers and small owner-occupiers, plus a significant number of landless labourers. Case D traces the experience of a new migrant workers' union whose members are seasonal wage earners in agriculture but who, for the rest of the year, work communal lands as sharecroppers, tenant farmers or small owner-occupiers or are landless labourers. Case E is devoted to a relatively young and weak national federation of provincial peasant organisations and of "enterprise" unions operating in a situation where no significant agrarian reform is taking place.

In Part II examples of ten different types of special service are examined: savings and loan schemes, purchasing and marketing schemes, consumer co-operative and similar schemes, housing schemes, community development, technical agrarian services, educational services, health care schemes, child care centres and legal services. The experiences of two or more rural workers' organisations are examined with respect to each of these ten types of special service.

The treatment of all 15 case studies follows the same pattern: *background* of the example; *special needs of members* requiring special services; *project plans and methods*; and *observations and conclusions*.

Background. In this section of each case study, as much background information as is available and pertinent is presented. Wherever possible, the following topics are included: age and relative strength of the union; categories of rural workers who are members; amount of dues that the members pay; average income of members by groups; dues paid by the lowest-income group of members, expressed as a percentage of their income; percentage of rural workers organised; situation of the economy in which the union functions; and general policies of the union.

Special needs of members. The need or needs of members to be met by the special services provided by their union are examined as regards: the reasons why the need cannot be furthered and defended by the traditional methods of negotiation and/or representation; the extent and degree of the need; and the way in which the union determined the order of priority of needs to be met by special services.

Project plans and methods. Information is presented on: any survey work done by the union; the content of the special service to be rendered; whether the special service is financed out of the general funds of the union or by special payments from the participating members; administrative matters; whether the service was initiated with only union resources or in conjunction with others; the extent of participation by others, and how this was obtained; whether the special service has become or can become self-financing; whether the need of members was or was not met by the special service.

Observations and conclusions. Under the case study method, these are normally left to the reader. However, much more detailed information is usually available than in the examples presented. More important, the purpose of this book is "guidance"—for members, officers and officials [1] of rural workers' organisations, or for those who may be called upon to offer, or who are interested in offering, assistance to rural workers' organisations in the development of special services. Therefore, any observations and conclusions which seem to offer guidance are put forward in this section of each case study.

Finally, Part III of the book provides useful advice on planning and operating special services.

Note. Whenever money matters have been referred to in the text the amounts involved have been given in NUs—national units of currency. The figures used are the actual figures for the national currency: for example, if the organisation studied in Case A had been in India, the figures quoted on p. 11 would have been in Indian rupees. Thus it is important to appreciate that whilst the NUs are constant and comparable within each case study, they are not comparable between one case study and another.

The main reason for this method of presentation is to discourage the reader from making comparisons with his own or an international currency and with his own standards of income and living. Comparisons of incomes are meaningless without a full knowledge of the respective costs of living, the spending habits of national and local cultures, the number

---

[1] The term "officer" is used throughout to denote voluntary workers elected to office; the term "official" is used to denote a paid member of the staff of the organisation (who may be either appointed or elected).

of hours worked to earn the income, deductions from pay, taxation and (in some countries) additions to incomes from social security funds. It can be taken for granted that the incomes of the members in each of the case studies (all of which are from developing countries) are markedly less than the national average, and in almost all cases are also markedly less than the incomes of industrial workers in their countries. These are factors which, it is frequently argued, make it impossible for rural workers to build and run an independent organisation and to provide successful special services through their organisation. The examples here show what has been achieved, in a form which can readily be measured in relation to the incomes of the members of the organisation in question.

Part I

*Case studies of rural workers'
organisations*

Case studies of rural workers' organisations

Case A: An organisation of plantation workers

Background

The members of this national rural workers' organisation are wage earners working on plantations. The workers are about evenly divided between male and female and many households have two or more wage earners. The illiteracy rate is about 20 per cent, mainly among older workers.

The union has been in existence for over 20 years and has a membership of well over 12 .000, covering about 80 per cent of the workers on some 2,000 plantations. The lowest-paid group of workers has an average income of NU 104 a month, or NU 1,248 a year, while the highest-paid group of workers has an average income of about NU 200 a month, or NU 2.400 a year.[1] The dues payable to the union are at the flat rate of NU 3 a month, which represents just under 3 per cent of the average income of the lowest-paid group and about 1.5 per cent of the income of the highest-paid group. These dues provide the union with an annual income of over NU 4.5 million.

As the union represents four-fifths of the plantation workers and is supported by a membership which, in the case of the members with the lowest incomes, pays dues amounting on average to over 2 per cent of those incomes, it is recognised by the employers, by government, by political parties and by society as a whole as the local and national "voice" of the country's plantation workers. The union is consequently able to further and defend the interests of its members very effectively through the traditional methods of trade unions: by collective bargaining with an employers' federation and with independent employers; by representation on a tripartite (government, unions, employers) joint national labour advisory council; and by pressure-group activities within the society as a whole. Yet, in developing countries, not even strong unions can further and defend all the interests of their members in these traditional ways; they must also develop special methods of satisfying their members' special needs.

[1] NU = national units of currency; see the explanation given in the introduction, p. 6.

Special needs of members

The members of this union have many special needs that have not been met through negotiations with employers or representations to government. Two of the most important of these needs relate to unemployment and to education.

Unemployment in the country's plantation sector is the result of a number of factors. First, technological changes have reduced by 16 per cent the number of workers needed to work the same acreage of land as before. Second, as a result of crop diversification, many of the new crops require only 50 per cent of the labour input of the crops they have replaced. Third, many plantations have been and are being sold to be divided up or urbanised. A fourth factor is the high birth rate in the plantation sector.

The educational and training needs of the members include both those of the adult members and those of their children. The unemployed or displaced workers in the plantations, having been trained to work only for the plantation sector of the economy, lack the skills needed to take jobs in other industries. Education beyond the primary level (six years of schooling) is not possible for most of the workers' children. On many estates, even primary schools are not provided and the distance to the nearest school is too great. Providing for their children's education in distant towns and cities is beyond the means of the average worker. Even those children who reach reasonably high levels of education have no specialised training that would enable them to obtain jobs outside the plantations.

Project plans and methods

After much research and investigation, the union decided to form a separate, but union-operated, organisation through which it would be able to attack the problem of unemployment among its members. The union had at first thought of forming a "union co-operative"—a co-operative limited to union members.[1] This is permitted under the law

---

[1] A trade union is by nature a "closed" association, in that it exists to serve the interests of a defined group of workers. Not anyone can be a member—the only workers who can join a union are those who fall within the membership definition set out in the union rules. On the other hand, a fundamental principle of the co-operative movements of many countries is that they shall be "open" societies—anyone who so wishes may become a member of the co-operative. Where this principle is also laid down in a country's legislation on co-operatives, a workers' organisation cannot establish a registered co-operative and at the same time restrict its membership and benefits to its union members. Occasionally unions do establish co-operatives which are open to all, but naturally they generally seek to find ways and means of providing this special service in such a way that it is available only to members of the union. In those cases where the union decides upon, and the law allows, the establishment of a formal co-operative, the latter has all the characteristics of operation, management and membership control of the country's co-operatives. If, on the other hand, the union is unable (or does not wish) to establish a formal co-operative, it may nevertheless itself undertake a co-operative-type activity based on its own structure and member-

governing registration of co-operatives in some countries but not under this country's laws. Accordingly, it therefore formed a "trading corporation".

Trading corporation

While the union itself owns no shares in this corporation, only union members are entitled to buy shares. With the funds raised by the sale of shares to members, the union has been able to undertake many activities to set up job-creating activities or maintain present jobs for members. In some cases it has done so in collaboration with others; in other cases the trading corporation has been the sole sponsor. The biggest scheme to date is a textile mill set up in a province where unemployment has been particularly acute. In a joint venture with the provincial government and a large textile company, a mill has been built which produces both yarn and finished goods and which employs about 2.000 workers. Acting alone, the corporation has started a daily general newspaper in another province. Plans are also under way in various provinces for container manufacturing, a plastics factory, the marketing of agricultural products, distribution companies and transport services. The union, relying on its experiences with the projects it has undertaken, hopes to start at least two new enterprises which will create new jobs in each province of the country.

With a view to helping some of the members in their present jobs, the trading corporation purchased two 2.000-acre plantation estates which were going to be subdivided by the owners. This action saved several hundred jobs for members.

The union-operated corporation also assisted in the formation of a national workers' bank by subscribing a substantial percentage of the share capital. It is hoped that, through the savings of all categories of workers throughout the country, the workers' bank will be able, among other activities, to lend money for starting up new industries which will create even more jobs.

Multi-purpose society

This union has also started a second scheme—a national multi-purpose society, through which it plans to buy up smaller estates as they come up for sale. The society has already purchased one 500-acre estate on which it will develop housing programmes and cottage industries, as well as land settlement schemes enabling unemployed members to build houses and to farm their own land. The housing scheme and the cottage

---

ship. Whilst the end objective of either method is the same (that of providing a special service to members), the operational principles differ greatly. For further information on the internationally agreed standards in relation to co-operatives, see the ILO's Co-operatives (Developing Countries) Recommendation, 1966 (No. 127).

industries will create employment and the land settlement schemes will provide an ideal method of reducing unemployment as no new training is required for the plantation workers. The first estate purchased under this scheme is in an area of acute unemployment, and the union intends that the society will concentrate its activities on such areas in the future.

Vocational institute

This special service is concerned with both unemployment and the training needs of members. The union's commercial projects created many skilled and semi-skilled jobs which an untrained unemployed plantation worker would not be able to undertake. In co-operation with a provincial government and an international vocational education institute, a facility has been established to train the unemployed and the children of plantation workers in the skills needed for the union's own enterprises and for other industries being set up by public and private enterprises.

Other educational services

Another educational service that also attacks the problem of unemployment is provided by the union itself under its adult education programme: courses in family planning are conducted throughout the plantations in the country. The union also has a system of scholarships and of study loans for the higher education of members' children. In addition, the union operates two hostels in the country's capital city (where the university is located) to provide inexpensive accommodation for students who are children of members. Under its adult education programme, the union has lowered and continues to lower the illiteracy rate among members and their families. Because distances to towns and in many cases to schools are great in the rural sector, the union has started a scheme intended to equip every estate with a reasonably good library.

Savings scheme

Early in its projects of special services to members, this union started a monthly savings scheme which was promoted by education and publicity campaigns and traditional slogans about "saving every pay-day". In this country, as in many other developing countries, it is not the custom among rural workers to save in anticipation of needs; they tend to borrow money at very high interest rates to meet needs as they arise. However, the savings scheme, backed up by the very important educational programmes and publicity, is working so well that, in only three years, a position has been reached where one-half of the members are each saving NU 10 a month: this, on an annual basis, gives aggregate savings amounting to well over NU 7 million. In addition to taking the members out of the hands of the money-lenders, these savings are used by the national economy for investments—the prime need of developing countries. Moreover, once the members had got into the habit of saving, the union was able to sell them shares in its trading corporation. The corporation is currently paying a 15 per cent annual dividend on these shares.

Legal and legal-administrative services

The union provides all members with complete legal services and makes no charge if the case concerns the member's pay, hours of work, grievances, accidents, entitlements from employer or government, and so on. If the case is purely personal and in no way related to work, the charges made are much lower than the normal legal fees. The union has been able to set up this service by reaching an agreement with the law firms it retains for its own legal affairs.

Co-operative food-growing

In addition to providing its members with the normal type of consumer services, the union launched a campaign to persuade members to grow their own food on a co-operative basis. A substantial proportion of the members' wages is spent on foodstuffs, which are always increasing in price. The land is available or can be negotiated from the employers on most estates, and the union intends, through education and publicity campaigns, to make this scheme a permanent feature of the plantations. As this country, like many other developing countries, imports a considerable amount of food every year, the idea has received support from the government. Under this scheme, participating members raise their real wages while the money which does not leave the country to pay for imported food can be made available for national development activities.

Observations and conclusions

This case has been chosen to illustrate a union s services to workers who are wage earners: but, if the choice fell on this particular union rather than on some other union just as large and as effective in furthering and defending the interests of its members, it was partly because the membership of this union does not include a large proportion of highly skilled and trained labour. This feature of the membership is reflected in the average income of the highest-paid group: at NU 200 a month, this is only twice the average income of the lowest-paid group. Where a great deal of processing of the production takes place on the plantation or near by (as is frequently the case in, for example, the sugar industry), there are several levels of skill and training involved, and the highest-paid group, although small, an receive four or five times as much income as the lowest. In such a situation, it is often claimed that the presence of more educated workers means faster and more effective development of the union because of the higher average education of the membership. Whatever the merits of the argument, the present case demonstrates that, despite insufficient educational and other facilities, agricultural wage earners in developing countries can nevertheless form strong and effective unions.

This case was also selected because of the availability of statistics on wages, which made it possible to calculate that the union dues paid by the lowest income group represent almost 3 per cent of their income. Furthermore, since both the number of members and their annual dues were known, it has also been possible to establish that the income of the union that is available for the provision of negotiating, representational and special services to members amounts, as already noted, to millions of NUs. The twin factors of a large number of members and a sound level of union dues in relation to members' incomes are of crucial importance. If the workers in this case had been split into two or more unions or if the level of union dues in relation to members' incomes had not been sound, the total union income would not have been sufficient to make it possible for the union to embark on some of its special services.

Because it represents 80 per cent of the workers in the industry, the union was able to obtain the co-operation of the employers and of government when it began tackling the special needs of members, especially since the needs were employment and education and training. Unions owning enterprises or trading corporations, whether directly or through members, do exist in different parts of the world, though they are not common. The important point is that the enterprises are not ends in themselves but only a means of creating employment for unemployed members. Possibly of even greater significance is the multi-purpose society because, with its cottage industries and land-settlement schemes, it brings services to the non-wage-earning rural workers. It is also a method of keeping the lands of the plantations under labour-intensive use, thereby maintaining employment.

Among the services which a rural wage earners' organisation of more modest size and strength may be in a position to offer to members are the various adult education programmes and the savings scheme campaign and operation. The co-operative food-growing scheme merits the serious consideration of all plantation unions, particularly where the food of the members is expensive and imported.

Rural workers include wives and mothers like these Iranian women...

Case B: A national federation of peasant farmers

Background

This rural workers' organisation is a national federation; most of its members are peasants, though its membership also includes some rural wage earners. The organisation is some 30 years old. The membership is very large and represents a very high proportion of the country's total number of peasants. The number of local or base units affiliated to the national federation runs into several hundreds. The federation is recognised as the national "voice" of the peasants.

As with all peasant unions, the main concern of this national federation is with agrarian reform. Based on a political decision taken several years ago, a wide-ranging agrarian reform programme has been and is being carried out: it is on a very much larger scale than the agrarian reforms in the countries referred to in the other case studies of rural workers' organisations in this book.

Like all peasant unions, this national federation insists on the participation of the peasants and their leaders in agrarian reform as part of the reform. Accordingly, the federation participates actively in all the agrarian reform institutions, bodies, commissions and banks. In addition to participation in the agrarian reform, this peasant union's policy is to lay much emphasis on the need for continuing militancy during and after agrarian reform. For this reason, it began some years ago to accept as affiliates associations of settlers, co-operative enterprises and associations and other economic organisations that are created or fostered by agrarian reform. The peasant thus has dual membership: in his economic unit, and in a trade union. The federation has observed that, when the peasant is a member only of his local economic unit, his interests tend to be determined by the agrarian reform technicians because he does not have the advantage of membership of a national organisation which he can influence for the furthering and defending of his interests as he sees them.

The dues payable to the national federation consist of 25 per cent of any dues received by the affiliated local units or organisations. The total amount of dues received has in fact proved to be small. As a participant in agrarian reform, the national federation receives an annual subsidy. In addition, to help to meet the expenses of the traditional services to members, the federation charges 2 per cent on the loans or credits that members receive through the federation from the agrarian reform banks.

Special needs of members

Even where a programme of agrarian reform is under way, a peasant union may have to provide services for many other needs. The national federation identified several problems which its members were having to face: the high cost of agricultural chemicals and farm machinery, the wide fluctuations in the price the peasants were receiving for one of their main crops (rice), the high cost of processing and marketing the rice, and the lack of agricultural machinery to work the peasants' lands.

Project plans and methods

The federation set up an advisory committee to investigate methods of overcoming these difficulties. The committee recommended the setting up of three companies or enterprises: one to import and distribute agricultural machinery and chemicals: another to acquire a rice-processing plant; and a third to hire out heavy agricultural equipment, such as mechanical rice harvesters, to associations of settlers and co-operatives.

Supply enterprise

The members contributed 10 per cent of the capital with which the supply enterprise was set up, the remainder being borrowed from banks. The company's original capital has multiplied several times over the years. This enterprise has been importing, servicing, repairing and re-building agricultural machinery and also manufacturing animal-drawn machinery. The federation reached an agreement with the agrarian institute and agrarian bank whereby any government assistance to peasants for purchasing agricultural machinery would be channelled through this supply enterprise.

Processing company

The processing company bought a rice-threshing plant, the cost of which was financed by a loan to the federation and a cash transfer from the supply enterprise. The operation of this plant put an end to a series of conditions on which the rice companies had been insisting so that they could buy rice from the peasants at low prices. At the same time, the plant brought high-quality products to the markets at fair prices, thereby forcing commercial enterprises to lower their prices. However, the federation learned that maintaining this service in a highly competitive business would require a much larger capital investment than was available to the enterprise or to the federation. Accordingly, after a few years of operation, it decided to give up this service and sold the plant to the agrarian bank.

Harvesting service

The harvesting service was set up to provide settlement associations and co-operatives with mechanical rice-harvesting equipment; but experience has shown that this type of machine service enterprise is best set up within the largest settlements themselves instead of operating it, as the federation has been doing, from provincial capitals.

Marketing company

The federation later established a fourth enterprise. This is a marketing company designed to eliminate the many middlemen between the peasant producing the foodstuffs and the urban consumer. Of the capital with which this enterprise was started, about 57 per cent came from the federation, about 7 per cent each from two of the federation's other enterprises and about 14 per cent each from the agrarian bank and a national foundation. The marketing company operates in two cities. It also sells food, tools and agricultural materials to the peasants in the receiving centres in the countryside to which members bring their produce to be sold in the city. It took three years for the marketing company to break even financially. The costs of the operation are covered by a 2 per cent charge to the peasants on goods sold.

None of the federation's enterprises is designed to make profits: their purpose is to service the special needs of members and member organisations. Any capital accumulations are used to increase services or are transferred to other enterprises to start new services. The federation has several strong regional committees and base units which have also started their own enterprises.

Observations and conclusions

This rural workers' organisation illustrates a peasant union's special services to its members in a country in which an important agrarian reform programme is being carried out. As part of its participation in the reform, the peasant union itself is given access to credits and grants which enable it to start enterprises to service the special needs of peasants for which considerable amounts of capital are required.

Much careful study and analysis by the federation went into the selection of methods to meet the special needs of members. But even the best laid plans need to be constantly re-examined while the projects are being carried out. Although successful in its original purpose, the processing company would have required very large increases of capital investment in order to remain competitive with similar commercial operations. Had the federation not decided to withdraw from this field, it would have put all other enterprises and even the federation itself in jeopardy. This would have been too high a price to pay for any activity servicing the special needs of some members only.

The special harvesting service illustrates a different kind of situation, and one that frequently arises. The federation learned through its own operation that there was another way of having this service provided which would not directly involve the federation itself. This situation can come about in almost any type of special activity and, when it does, a decision needs to be taken (as it was in this case) to phase out the activity. A rural workers' union should not engage in or continue in special services which can be done as well or better by others. Put another way, a union begins or continues a special service only because there is no other organisation that can or will provide the needed service to members. Special services are a means to an end, not an end in themselves.

The federation's enterprise for importing and distributing agricultural machinery is an example of a co-operative type of purchasing activity which can service the needs of peasant members by reducing prices for agricultural materials and which, when tied to a government programme of low-cost credits, can put fertilisers, improved seed and even some mechanisation into the hands of many more peasants than would otherwise be possible.

The federation's marketing company actually performs a double service: on the one hand, a service to producers by marketing the crops of peasant members and, on the other, a service to consumers by selling food and other items at reduced prices to the peasants. An important point to note here is that, since the two services are performed at the same produce-collecting centres, there are savings in the cost of operations.

Case C: A local organisation of sharecroppers, tenant farmers, small owner-occupiers and landless day labourers

Background

The members of this rural workers' organisation are sharecroppers, tenants and small owner-occupiers, together with a substantial number of landless day labourers. Those who do have land to work also work as day labourers when the opportunity to do so arises. This union is quite new and is at present working in only one district of one of the country's provinces. The union is being financially subsidised in its early stages by an international workers' organisation. With the exception of wage earners on some plantations, the rural workers in this country are not organised; however, the union hopes that it will spread within the province and eventually become a national union.

The policy of this union is to further and defend the interests of its members (the rural poor) in the following ways: by applying pressure on the government for more rural reform; by demanding the participation of the rural poor and their representatives in rural reform agencies and bodies; by taking measures designed to ensure that any rural develop- · ment funds and programmes coming from government, international or private agencies do reach the rural poor rather than the rural élite; and by developing special projects to service the special needs of the members.

The members of this union are among the poorest rural workers in the world. The present membership covers an area of some 20 villages inhabited by approximately 2,500 families. Of these families, 18 per cent are those of the landless day labourers, 19 per cent work from 1 to 2 hectares[1] of land ("small peasants", under the government classification), 51 per cent work less than 1 hectare of land ("marginal peasants"). The average income per head is approximately NU 270 a year in the families of landless labourers, NU 320 a year in marginal peasant families and NU 380 a year in small peasant families, the average family annual incomes being, respectively, NU 1,325, NU 1,895 and NU 3,434. If the income of the "small peasant" family is much larger than that of the "marginal peasant" family, it is not only because it has more land but also because the sons apparently tend to stay longer in their families and thus to augment the family income whenever they find work.

There is a very high rate of illiteracy in the area, particularly among the women. Although only 29 per cent of the men are literate (the national rate being 40 per cent), the literacy rate among women is as low as 4 per cent (as against a national rate of 19 per cent). Up to the present the union has organised 40 per cent of the families in this area. These 1,000 families are each paying NU 6 a year to the union in dues.

The union has so far concentrated its efforts on measures designed to ensure that any rural development funds and programmes shall reach the membership and on developing services to meet the special needs of its members.

Special needs of members

The severity of the rural problem having prompted the government and international agencies to carry out research in the area, the resulting statistical data are available to the union. The union has also carried out research of its own. Working through the union's 20 village committees, the union's officers have drawn up a long list of the needs of the members which might be met by special union projects and services. Through their village committees, the members have listed the needs in an order of priority.

The economic needs both of the marginal and small peasants and of the landless labourers are basically the same: their common need is for more work to produce more income. Both groups suffer from considerable underemployment. For the peasants, the need is to enable them to get more out of the land they work, as there is no spare land for them in this area. For the labourers, the need is to create more jobs for them.

---

[1] 1 hectare = 2.47 acres.

Both groups are in need of legal, administrative, health and educational services.

Project plans and methods

With a committee functioning in each of the 20 villages, with two full-time field representatives and with some volunteer help, particularly from the unemployed or underemployed youth of member families, the union had sufficient staff to begin providing the special services. The field representatives are trade unionists drawn from the rural poor who have been given special training in agrarian, technical and administrative subjects. [1]

Subsidies and low-interest loans are provided to small and marginal peasants under government programmes. However, owing to the heavy hand of bureaucracy (the signatures of six to ten officials in different parts of the district are needed in each case), the cost of processing applications (fees have to be paid for most signatures), qualification restrictions (to receive certain benefits, the peasant has to have 10 to 25 per cent cash in hand) and the ignorance of the peasants, none of the poorer peasants was receiving any of these benefits. Although several private agencies working in this country have been trying to assist in the development of the rural areas and of the living standards of the rural poor, they have failed to develop methods of ensuring that their help actually reaches the rural poor.

The basic plan and method of the union was to combine its own resources (the village committees, the volunteer help, the trained field representatives and the officials) with the resources available from government and private programmes and thus to operate the special services for members' needs.

Fertiliser

Most members cannot afford the cash investment to buy the amount of fertiliser required to increase their agricultural production. The union obtained from the authorities a licence in its own name to procure and distribute fertiliser. The members need loans to buy the fertiliser. The various forms for applying for fertiliser loans from the development bank take several weeks to prepare and have signed and certified in various places if the members undertake this task themselves; there is also a cash expenditure of over NU 20 (5-7 per cent of the average income per head) for various fees, stamps, photographs, and so on. In addition, many members could not find the two guarantors needed for this type of loan. The union established an "application processing" service for members. About five man-hours were needed to complete the

---

[1] See also below, p. 57.

necessary forms for each application; but the members' out-of-pocket expenses were reduced from NU 20 to NU 4. The union officials also took the forms to the appropriate authorities. In addition, the union officials, while not acting as guarantors, were eventually accepted by the bank at least as a substitute for one guarantor. Most of the loans received for fertiliser by members ranged between NU 200 and NU 300 each, although some were for as little as NU 24. Through this union service 650 members received loans in one season. In almost all cases, they had never received a loan before the union was organised.

Irrigation

The soil and the climate of this area make it possible to raise more than one crop a year; in fact, all the larger farmers in the area do so, by using irrigation water from tube-wells. None of the peasants who are members of the union can finance the cost of a tube-well and pump. However, government low-interest loans are available for irrigation projects. In this case, too, an application-processing service was set up by the union and has resulted up to the present in the installation of 40 tube-wells and pumps for individual members and groups of members. Some of the peasants could obtain and repay the loans for an individual well, but the individual holdings of the marginal peasants are too small to make them eligible for such a loan, which they would not be able to repay. The union has had to spend much time on education and discussions to secure acceptance of the idea of joint ownership of a well for the use of three or four adjoining holdings. The demonstrated benefits to those who were convinced and who have adopted the system should reduce the need to persuade other members in the future.

The first few installations of wells were undertaken by a contractor. The union has now acquired its own (very limited) well-boring equipment and is developing a service to members which also provides employment for the membership. The union has also purchased some pumps on behalf of members and, as the union spreads to other districts, its increased purchasing power should enable the membership to save considerably on the cost of equipment.

Eligibility for subsidies

The district in which this union is organised is one of those covered by a special development agency of the national government for small, marginal and landless peasants. The programmes of this agency provide the rural poor with development incentives in the form of subsidies for fertilisers, tube-wells, pumps, agricultural implements, milk cows, sheep, goats and poultry. In order to be eligible for subsidies, the rural poor have to be identified and certified as falling below certain income levels.

This work involved the union in by far its heaviest processing or legal-administrative servicing operation; but it was essential to make sure that government rural development funds did actually reach the rural poor. For this purpose, the union arranged for volunteers to go to the members' homes to complete the forms and then to pass them through all the various authorities. In the early stages of the scheme about 800 members (four-fifths of the membership) received their identity cards in this manner, and about 150 of the poorest among them received an aggregate subsidy of NU 8,000 for fertiliser, or an average of about NU 50 per member assisted. This is equivalent to one-fifth of the average annual income per head of the poorest group of members.

Soil testing

No peasant member of the union has ever had a soil test of the land he works. With a view to determining the right types of fertiliser and to ascertain the correct rates of application for optimum production on members' land, volunteers took a total of 150 soil samples in five out of the 20 villages covered by the union. This programme will eventually cover all the 20 villages.

Fee reductions

Almost any transaction relating to landholdings in this area requires certification by a village revenue official. Although the official certification fee is NU 0.5, some officials charge whatever they think they can get, a sum varying between NU 2 and NU 10. Before the union was organised, these officials had very little certification business. However, with the activity generated by the special services of the union, there are now many documents to be certified. The union has been able to arrange for the revenue officials to come to the union office at mutually agreed times, when as many as 50 documents are certified at one sitting at the nominal official rate, i.e. NU 0.5 per document. Thus the officials gain, and so do the members.

Household dairying

The union survey work indicates a need to improve the milk output of local cows. A district unit for breed improvement is being established. While this area is not suitable for large-scale dairy farming owing to a dearth of fodder, the union has a project for supplementing members' incomes through milk production. Under this project, 50 member families in one of the larger villages were each to be provided with one cow of an improved variety. Seventeen members and three officials of the union received four days of intensive training in household dairying at a national dairy institute. The cost of the training was paid partly by the union and partly by a private agricultural agency. The cost of the cows is met from bank loans to members arranged by the union.

Rickshaws

While all the families have special needs, it is particularly difficult to develop programmes for the group of landless day labourers because the funding of most projects through bank loans requires the participants to have land to work. The union has several special projects for this group. The necessary research has been done but the application of some of the projects will have to wait until the union covers more districts and hence has more funds coming in from members.

Some special services for this group have nevertheless already been started. Member labourers are used in all union projects. Some members asked the union for help in purchasing cycle rickshaws so that they might earn a living by transporting passengers. Banks require a 25 per cent down payment on loans for rickshaws, which cost about NU 1,000. The union was able to negotiate loans with a bank for a down payment of only 10 per cent, or NU 100. Three members were able to "find" the necessary NU 100 but the union later discovered that these members had borrowed the down payment from money-lenders at 120 per cent interest! The union then initiated a programme of lending the 10 per cent down payment to members directly. Some 20 unemployed members have so far bought rickshaws under this project; they have repaid the whole of the 10 per cent down payment received from the union and are maintaining their payments to the bank. These members can earn NU 5 to NU 10 a day.

Woollen blankets scheme

On the basis of government statistics and its own survey, the union was able to form a clear picture of the cottage industries existing in the area, of those that seemed "over-crowded" and of those offering the best prospect of successful development. The first endeavour to create employment in this way is a scheme under which woollen blankets would be manufactured by unemployed members in their homes. Using its research figures and its demonstrated ability to develop and administer earlier projects, the union sought from a national private aid foundation an interest-free loan to be deposited in a district bank, which was sufficient for a down payment on a much larger loan to finance the necessary equipment. The first step has been to select five traditional artisans and five unemployed members for special training in this industry. The bank will then lend the needed amounts to these ten members for their equipment and materials. As soon as this has been shown to be economically sound, the project can be expanded through the bank and by using the five artisans as teachers.

Sewing scheme

The same statistics and union research used for the woollen blanket manufacturing scheme led to a decision to start a cottage industry scheme for making clothing and embroideries. In one village 25 women are interested. A large national sewing-machine manufacturer has agreed to provide a mobile training school for the necessary training and is ready to provide machines on easy instalment terms. Again, if this project proves to be economically sound, it can be applied to other villages.

Domestic poultry keeping

This special service to the membership is aimed at supplementing the income of the poorest members—those who are landless or have less than half a hectare to till. From 10 to 20 chickens, three to four months old, are supplied to qualifying members. These chickens start laying within two to three months. Even the poorest members can provide shelter and feed for the chickens. The scheme is based on a revolving fund: the money spent will return to be used again in the same way. Members return to the union 15 eggs per bird in the first laying year and 10 eggs per bird in the second laying year. The eggs are sold by the union and the money returned to the "poultry fund" to be used again in the same scheme. The hope is to multiply domestic poultry keeping as a means of supplementing both income and food throughout the area. Up to the present, about 2,500 birds have been supplied to 120 member families.

Fish production

One official of this union has been trained at a government course in fish-raising techniques. Fish is an important item of the diet in this area even though it is far from the natural source of this food. The union identified seven villages with small ponds or tanks for fish production. Twelve families are raising fish from 12,000 fingerlings (seed fish) obtained by the union from the government. If successful, this scheme can be spread throughout these and other villages.

Legal-administrative services

Although this special service has already been described under various projects, its importance is such that it also calls for separate treatment. None of the officials of this union is trained in law, but, as has been seen, several of the most important projects involved a great deal of work with applications, forms, land certificates and other legal or semi-legal documents. As short one- or two-day courses can suffice to train staff to handle this work, literate unemployed youngsters were trained as volunteers to do some of it. The figures of literacy rates already given indicate clearly that, if the union did not provide this service. most of the members would not receive the loans or benefits which they need and to which they are entitled.

Health services

The health services in the area are in many ways inadequate; but a more important point is that, owing to poverty and ignorance, members do not use them. Surveys show that there is virtually no understanding of preventive medicine and health care. It is clear, therefore, that there must be some servicing of the special needs of members in this field. The union has plans for action to be taken when it is strong enough. In the meantime. the union's milk project will bring milk into an area where almost no infant or child now receives it. Furthermore, by means of drawings and simple charts, as well as short talks at meetings, some fundamental principles of preventive health care are already being brought to the knowledge of members and their families.

Education

The special needs of members for all types of education make this a necessary future project. The union's policy in these early stages is "education by action" and "leadership training by example". However, some full-time officials and many volunteer workers have followed special courses and received on-the-job training in such subjects as trade unionism. legal-administrative servicing, irrigation. fertilisers, soil testing, household dairying, fish farming and domestic poultry keeping. Many members have also received this training. as well as training in cottage industry skills. This considerable amount of educational work was accomplished in a single year.

Observations and conclusions

This rural workers' organisation was chosen for several reasons: the amount of specific data available on the actual economic and social situation of the members; the very low level of income of the members; the substantial proportion of landless labourers in the membership; the absence of any scope for land reform in an area where there are no very large or absentee landowners and where there is no land that is not being used; the recent development of rural trade unionism, other than for plantation workers. in this part of the world; the demonstration of the value of surveys; the simple use of a revolving fund; the number and variety of special services provided; the employment as volunteers of unemployed or underemployed youths from members' families in the servicing programmes; and the demonstration of the value of reputation—one or two successful projects by a rural union greatly improve the union's ability to find resources for further services.

This case is of particular interest as a demonstration of what might be done in other developing countries where rural unions are yet to be organised: the immediate and effective combination of this union's policy of taking action to ensure that any rural development funds and resources coming from government, international or private agencies do in fact reach the rural poor with the union's other policy of developing projects which meet the special needs of its members. It is in this way that this union has been able to do so much so quickly. The reputation that it gained after a few successful projects enabled it to generate resources directly from members and from local banks.

But above all, this case strikingly illustrates what an organisation "of, by and for" the rural poor can do. Many of the financial and technical resources that the union utilised in its special services to members were available before the union was organised. Yet none of them reached the rural poor—indeed, if this union had not been organised, it is unlikely that any of the rural poor would ever have benefited from those resources.

This union carefully planned every new service, always weighing the expressed needs of the members against its own resources and personnel and any available outside resources. By stretching to the utmost its limited manpower and finances, the union accomplished much very quickly; but it deliberately refrained from trying to do what would have destroyed it.

There is one negative observation to be made. It appears, from the data available, that this union has not been separating the expenses for its general operations from the costs of its special services to the members. Some members have been receiving services which other members do not need or do not use. The expenses incurred by the union in providing these services should be paid for by the members receiving them and should not be charged to the union's general funds, which are fed from the dues of all members. A case in point is the processing of applications and forms for irrigation loans. The average time spent by the union on this work was five man-hours per application. As only 40 members out of the 1,000 members received this service, the considerable cost to the union of devoting 200 man-hours of work for the benefit of only a few members should be borne by those receiving the service. There are some rural unions which make a charge at a flat rate of 0.5 to 2 per cent (depending on the size of the loan) of any loans received through union processing. Other unions charge a flat fee based on their knowledge of their costs. If one or the other of these two systems were adopted, the cost of this special service to only 40 members would not be a charge borne by the dues paid by all members.

It is true that this particular union is not typical inasmuch as it is being subsidised in its early stages by the international labour movement; but it is equally true thàt, as this union grows in geographical scope and in the size of its membership, it will be able to operate with a much smaller numerical ratio of officials to members and will thus become self-supporting from the dues of members.

However, there is one very serious flaw in this union's operation. As noted earlier, the evidence from strong and effective unions of rural workers indicates the need for a union due equivalent to approximately 2 per cent of the income of the poorest members. In this case, the dues are far too low in relation both to the resources that the union must have in order to build itself up and maintain itself and to the capacity of the members to pay. As already mentioned, the union's present dues are at the rate of NU 6 a year for each member family and the average income per family of the lowest income group in the union—the landless labourers—is NU 1,325 a year. The poorest group is thus paying less than 0.5 per cent of its income in dues. There is no record of any rural workers' organisation being strong enough to further and defend the interests of its members with dues at such a low level. As was shown in another case, even the poorest can and do pay 2 per cent of their incomes to have their own workers' organisation.

Case D: An organisation of seasonal agricultural wage earners

Background

The overwhelming majority of the members of this rural workers' organisation are migrant seasonal wage earners. They come to work for four to six months a year in an area of about 750 square miles of intensive commercial agriculture. The lowest-paid field workers earn an average of NU 50 a month, while the tractor drivers earn an average of NU 125 a month. The majority of the lowest paid are either sharecroppers elsewhere in the country, whose land is not sufficient to feed their families, or small cultivators having the use of communal land but who, not having an ox and plough (which cost NU 300-400), come to work as wage earners to obtain the money required to meet this or other needs. All come to work without their families as the area is very unhealthy and hot and there is no housing. During the peak season there are between 100,000 and 150,000 workers. There are also 10,000 to 20,000 workers who are employed throughout the year.

There are between 2,000 and 3,000 employers in the area, of whom about 1,000 are members of a production and marketing co-operative. Most of the produce is intended for export. The area has been open to intensive commercial agriculture for only a few years, having been malaria-infested until an eradication programme was introduced.

With the exception of a few tractor repair-men in the town which serves this area, none of the workers had ever heard or a rural workers' organisation. The request to the national trade union centre [1] to help these agricultural workers to form a union was in fact made by the lorry drivers who carried supplies into and produce out of the area and who themselves belonged to a strong transport workers' organisation.

Special needs of members

In the organising campaign to form and register an area-wide union of agricultural workers, surveys were made to ascertain the existing wages and working conditions and to discover what the workers wanted most from a union. The surveys showed that the interests which the workers wanted furthered and defended were, in order of importance, as follows: to have their families notified if they died; to be buried according to the practice of their beliefs; to be paid, since a good many employers failed (often for a whole season) to pay their workers' wages; better medical services; and some housing, as well as recreational facilities when they went to town, which happened infrequently as they usually worked seven days a week in order to earn as much as possible during the season. There were no suggestions for improvements in wages, hours of work and working conditions. Apart from wanting to be paid the wages due to them, all their wants were for special services. Notification of a death to the family and burial according to desire are services that are relatively easy to establish and administer, once the union is functioning well. The provision of recreational facilities would be possible in the future. The really heavy task was the setting up of a medical scheme.

There is one 20-bed clinic for this whole area. The government staffs it with medical technicians; there are no doctors, simply because no doctor is available. The nearest hospital where there are doctors is 250 miles away, over roads which are closed for several months each year by rains and resulting damage. The rivers are contaminated with parasites. Poisonous snakes abound. The migrant workers come from a different climate and continue by custom and ignorance not to wear any head covering in the strong sunlight of a semi-desert area. During the peak season the numbers of sick and injured who can get as far as the clinic greatly exceed the clinic's capacity. Many more never reach the clinic. Less than 5 per cent of the employers (according to the surveys) have a medi-

---

[1] The term "national trade union centre" or "national centre" or "national confederation" is used to describe a national organisation which has as affiliates national workers' organisations of various occupations. In some countries there will be only one such centre; in others more than one, each having some political or sectoral affiliation.

cal technician of any grade or level in their employ. Although there are no firm figures on the annual death rate, it is clear from the first two wants referred to above that it is extremely high.

The organising campaign was successful and an area-wide union of some 15.000 members was registered. The executive committee of the union, with technical advice and assistance from an international trade secretariat [1] for rural workers, set up a "double-dues" system. All members pay the union NU 2 a month. These dues go into the union's "general fund" and are used for the normal operations of the union, which, it is planned, will include a large number of full-time field representatives with four-wheel drive vehicles, and for the costs of the traditional methods of furthering and defending the interests of the members. The members, as they become covered by the union medical scheme, will pay an additional NU 2 a month as "welfare" dues. This money goes into the union's "welfare fund" and can be spent only on the union medical scheme and other special services such as death notification, burial, recreational facilities and consumer activities.

The dues are equivalent to 2 per cent of the average income of the lowest-paid group of members.

Project plans and methods

The development of a union medical scheme that would be suited to the local situation called for much careful planning based on the collection of detailed information and on some financial and technical assistance to get the scheme started. The plan ultimately drawn up provided for small air-conditioned medical vans designed to operate in areas remote from medical facilities. Without the air-conditioning the vans, which have to remain at a standstill for hours at a time in the tropical sun, would soon become ovens. The back of the van is a well equipped, very small medical office with an examination table, packed with built-in basic medical equipment and supplies. The van is in effect a very small health clinic on wheels, intended to cope with illnesses and injuries up to a certain level of complexity and, in more serious cases, to prepare the patient for transfer to other facilities. A fully equipped van costs NU 40.000; but, through an international rural workers' organisation, one was obtained without charge from an international institute working with workers' organisations, while funds for technical assistance in starting this special service were obtained from an international development agency.

---

[1] The term "international trade secretariat" is used to denote the international organisation to which trade unions covering membership in a single trade or occupation are affiliated. In agriculture there are three main organisations of this kind: the International Federation of Plantation, Agricultural and Allied Workers (IFPAAW); the Trade Unions International of Agricultural, Forestry and Plantation Workers (TUIAFPW); and the World Federation of Agricultural Workers (WFAW).

The plan took account of the fact that it would not be possible to start a medical scheme that would immediately cover all members throughout the 750 square miles of the area. The scheme comes into operation in phases, the first phase covering roughly one-quarter of the area and of the membership. The scope of the next phase will depend on the experience gained in the first.

The plan shows the operating costs of the first phase as follows:

	NU/year	Percentage of total operating costs
Medical van (donated), NU 40,000; annual reserve for replacement after an estimated life of ten years and allowing for inflation	5 000	23
Van operation, fuel, maintenance, repair (based on actual experiences in the area) at NU 0.50/mile for an estimated annual mileage of 10,800 (60 a day for 180 days)	5 400	25
Mobile radios (donated), NU 4,000; ten-year reserve for replacement and allowing for inflation	500	2
Chief medical technician: salary and allowances	5 000	23
Two first-class technicians: salaries and allowances	6 000	27
Medicines and drugs: two-year supply donated (reserve for replacement will be started in the second year in the light of the first year's experience)	—	—
Total	21 900	100

If members worked for an average of only four months in the season (a low estimate), the union would receive NU 30,000 from 3,750 members paying NU 2 per month to the welfare fund. The figure of NU 30,000 (rather than NU 21,900) was chosen in order to allow a sufficient margin for an important item in any new and complicated project, i.e. "miscellaneous and unforeseen expenditure".

In addition, the union medical scheme includes plans for the establishment, in phases, of three one-room medical stations staffed by technicians strategically posted in the area, as well as for the renting of accommodation in the town; this is intended for the reception of members who need periods of rest and nourishment after treatment at

the government clinic (thus freeing beds and personnel at the clinic) or after treatment by the union medical technicians at the vans or field stations.

The plan as devised by the union has been accepted as meeting the conditions for assistance by the donor organisations, and the union expects to launch the first stage of the medical scheme at the start of the next peak agricultural season. The donors have also agreed to provide three additional medical vans if the first phase is successful.

The union welfare fund will provide sufficient funds not only for this medical scheme but also for much more in the way of necessary special services. If the union membership grows to 50,000 four-month seasonal workers and to 5,000 permanent workers, and if all members join the welfare scheme and pay NU 2 a month, the annual income of the welfare fund would amount to NU 500,000.

Before starting this project, the union spent much time on a fruitless investigation of ways and means of meeting this vital need of the membership by means of traditional methods. There is a government development plan with international assistance which calls for the construction of a large, fully equipped regional hospital within ten years. Should that plan be realised, it would be easy enough for the union's medical scheme to provide for payment to the hospital of all the costs charged to members using its facilities, possibly with negotiated contributions from the employers.

In the meantime, there are many workers who are in need of medical care from doctors and surgeons and who, without it, will not survive. The union is investigating the feasibility of a commercial arrangement with the few charter pilots operating out of the city 250 miles away whereby emergency cases could be flown out under the union's scheme.

Normally, union services paid for by members should be available only to members; but, in the locally prevailing situation, it would be socially and morally indefensible to confine the union's medical scheme to the members. Accordingly, the union will make its medical facilities available to employees, their families and all others in the area, as requested, at a charge of NU 10 per visit.

Observations and conclusions

Although this special service has not yet begun, it was chosen for inclusion in this book for several reasons. In the first place, it illustrates, with actual figures from the union's plan, a special service requiring heavy capital outlays on equipment (medical vans) which, though donated, requires provision for its replacement out of union income. If that provision were not made, not only would the medical scheme die with the equipment, but so would the union itself, because the members would be disillusioned by the loss of so vital and basic a service.

Buying through a consumer co-operative store in Papua New Guinea (above)

Housing scheme for plantation workers in Malaysia (below)

This case also illustrates the need for extensive information collection (much more was in fact done than has been described here) when considering any special service; also it shows how important it is, in order to get a special service started, to work out a plan on paper with all the supporting data, particularly when assistance is required from others.

This particular case illustrates, too, one way of tackling the organisation of services in the context of large-scale commercial agricultural operations in a very isolated area where the bulk of the workers are seasonal. There are many other similar places still waiting to be organised. This example should suggest, first, that no situation is as difficult as it may seem, and second, that, in dealing with such a situation, it is necessary to obtain experienced assistance from the national trade union centre and an international trade secretariat for rural workers.

It must be noted, however, that this medical scheme was designed for a particular situation. A medical scheme in a different situation would require much information collection and decisions based on the local realities.

Case E: A national federation of organisations of peasant farmers and plantation workers

Background

This rural workers' organisation is a national federation of provincial peasant organisations and of "enterprise" unions in sugar, banana, cocoa and mixed production plantations. The federation is about five years old. The peasant members are mainly sharecroppers and tenants. While exact statistics are not available, the average income of the poorest group of peasants is of the order of NU 1,000 a year, while that of the lowest-paid group of wage earners is about three times higher, i.e. NU 3,000 a year. The federation has a total membership of several thousands, evenly divided between peasants and wage earners.

The federation receives 70 per cent of the members' dues, the remaining 30 per cent going to the local unit—the provincial organisation in the case of peasant members and the enterprise union in the case of wage earner members. All members are on a double dues system: one due is payable annually and the other, monthly. The annual due is for a union card issued in each calendar year, for which all members pay NU 10. All members also pay NU 2 in monthly dues. Thus all members pay total dues of NU 34 a year, of which 70 per cent, or just under NU 24, goes to the national organisation. In practice, there is a collection problem within the peasant local units and between the national organisation and both the peasant and wage earner local units. At the moment, the national organisation receives the 70 per cent of the annual dues from most of the peasant local units but only from some of the wage earner local units.

This national organisation is a cross between a loose federation of autonomous local units and a centralised federation with centralised administration and policy. The organisation is striving to become fully centralised, receiving all dues in the first place and returning 30 per cent to the local units. The difficulty standing in the way of this arrangement is that the majority of the local units are much older than the national organisation. That the national organisation receives as much of the dues as it does is a reflection of its emphasis on service to the membership.

All officials of the national federation are constantly on the move in the field, giving traditional servicing in the form of legal advice and services; technical advice and representation in disputes between peasant members and landlords; technical advice and representation in collective bargaining between wage earner local units and the employers; and trade union education to all categories of member. Although not strong in terms of its potential membership or in financial resources, the national federation has been able to enlist the full support of the national trade union centre to which it is affiliated in its pressure-group activities on behalf of the rural workers.

Special needs of members

The membership of this national rural workers' organisation covers almost all categories of rural worker. The federation operates, however, in a developing economy which appears annually on the United Nations list of "least developed" countries and the national government has none of the assistance programmes for the rural poor that were so important and so well used by the rural workers' organisation described above in Case C.

Although the special needs of the members of this national federation are of every type imaginable, all the organisation's present resources are needed to provide the traditional trade union services to members.

Project plans and methods

The leadership of this federation wants to turn the idea of servicing the special needs of members into a method of so organising the rural workers that all members and all local units will pay their dues and that many times the present number of members will join. Instead of the more usual pattern of a rural workers' organisation beginning to service the special needs of members when it has sufficient resources of its own or in combination with others, this federation wants to use special services as a means of attracting new members paying their dues and thus increasing its resources.

At present, members turn to the national federation only when there is a serious problem, such as a group dispute with landlords or contract negotiations with an employer every two or three years. The new approach would include projects providing special services on a continuing basis and only to individual members whose dues are fully paid up and who belong to local units that are also up to date in their obligations to the national federation.

The federation's project calls for an operation in three stages. During the first phase, the international trade secretariat to which the federation is affiliated is assisting in some preliminary surveys to determine the services which would be of value to the largest numbers of members and which, at the same time, would be financially self-supporting. The second phase would be a technical study in depth of whatever projects came out of the first surveys, but would be undertaken by institutes or agencies specialising in co-operative activities. The purpose of the technical study would be to determine whether the projects selected in the first phase were really practical and economically feasible, bearing in mind that the costs of the service, once in full operation, must be no greater than the income generated by the project.

The final phase of this plan calls for the international trade secretariat to assist the federation in obtaining from interested international organisations the assistance and grants needed for starting the selected special projects.

Although the first phase has not yet been completed, two possible projects have already emerged. One is a federation-operated medical scheme somewhat similar to the one examined above under Case D. This would be of value only to the peasant members, as the wage earners receive medical services as part of the collective agreements negotiated with the employers. Since the peasants and wage earners are in separate local units, this presents no real problems. A secondary possible project would be some form of co-operative scheme whereby the federation would operate a service of lorries on a circular route between the principal cities, the plantation areas and the peasant areas. These lorries would bring from the cities items of secondary necessity for the wage earners (first-necessity items are provided at cost by employers under the collective agreements) and first-necessity items for the peasants; they would also transport peasant produce to the cities. The necessary consumer shops would be operated by the local wage earner units and peasant units in their areas and by urban workers' organisations in the cities. As this consumer-producer co-operative scheme is based largely on the transport of goods and produce, it would be economically feasible only if the lorries always carried loads, which in turn would be possible only if all segments of the "circular route" came under the scheme. It is hoped that, by eliminating the charges and profits of various middlemen between the city products and the rural workers and between the peasant produce and the city workers, the advantages to all would be sufficient to make all want to participate. This would keep the lorries always fully loaded and paying for themselves.

The federation is investigating other possible special projects and is obtaining technical assistance from two international development and co-operative agencies in evaluating the medical and the consumer-producer co-operative schemes.

Observations and conclusions

This federation has built up a solid (albeit still limited) base. It is receiving dues from local units in recognition of its demonstrated ability to provide traditional services of importance to both the peasant and wage earner members in the form of legal services and negotiating assistance. To provide even more of the traditional services to members, the federation needs to receive all dues on a regular basis from all members.

The collection of dues on a regular basis is a matter of vital administrative concern to all workers' organisations and can be a particular problem when the membership includes peasants who, unlike wage earners, do not receive cash incomes at regular intervals. This problem is inherent in, and seldom solved by, organisations having a federal structure, especially in the case of peasant federations. The formerly independent units which federate seldom agree to pay a sufficiently high proportion of their income to the federation's central administration to enable it to function as effectively as it should, having regard to the total number of affiliated members. However, should any of the special projects being investigated by this particular federation prove to be workable and also provide an important service desired by the membership, members and units will become and stay fully paid up in their dues to the federation in order to be eligible to receive those services.

To become effective in representing the rural workers with the government, the federation needs to be recognised as the "voice" of the rural workers, which means that it must greatly increase the proportion of the country's rural workers who are members. If any of the special projects proved to be important enough to the present membership to secure full and regular payment of dues, they could also be used as an inducement to more local units to join the federation, to more rural workers to join local units and to more rural workers to form new local units.

The federation, while at present limited in resources and membership, has used its demonstrated abilities, and a carefully planned step-by-step study of such special needs of members as it might be possible to service, to inspire the confidence of international co-operative and development agencies. These agencies are providing technical analyses and evaluations of possible projects which, if they prove positive, many result in the provision of financial and technical assistance in launching them. It should be noted that even rural workers' organisations with limited membership and resources and having no government assistance schemes for the rural poor which they can use, but which are providing some services to members, can enlist the co-operation of other organisations.

A final observation concerns the dues structure. If the whole of the charge for the annual union card went directly to the federation and if the charge were increased to 70 per cent of the present total dues (including the monthly dues), not only would the federation's income be better assured but the members' difficulty in having to pay dues every month would be overcome. It would still fall to the local units to collect the balance of 30 per cent due to them.

Part II

Case studies of special services

Case studies of special services

Savings and loan schemes

Background

The rural workers' organisation to be considered here is an "enterprise" union: its 12,000 or so members all work for the same large plantation company. The union is over 20 years old. The members are all wage earners. There is a very high percentage of skilled and trained workers, as the company runs processing facilities and railway, docks and shipping operations in addition to producing agricultural produce on the plantation. There is consequently a very wide difference in average income between the lowest-paid group of members, who earn NU 150 a month, and the highest-paid group, who earn over NU 600 a month—more than four times as much. Dues are at the flat rate of NU 3.20 a month for all members, which is equivalent to just over 2 per cent of the income of the lowest-paid workers and to 0.5 per cent of the income of the highest-paid workers.

The union has been very successful in representing the interests of members both with the employer in collective bargaining and with government in securing the passage of labour legislation; but, as in all developing countries, the members still had many needs which were not being met. The union, very early in its history, started projects to meet the special needs of members. It now has a union co-operative plan with six departments: housing, death benefits scheme, education, consumer co-operatives, holiday camp and—to be examined here—savings and loan. Union members are not required to join any of the six departments, but only union members may join these union schemes.

Special needs of members

As in many other developing countries, the rural areas are often plagued with money-lenders who charge exorbitant and sometimes illegal rates of interest. This union had many documented cases which it had taken to court in defence of members' interests. Some cases came before local magistrates who worked with the money-lenders. A typical loan would be for NU 500 when the worker wanted to borrow only NU 200; the interest was at 20 per cent a week and the worker was required to pay off the loan in total, not in part. Thus, in order to obtain the NU 200 he needed, the worker had to pay NU 100 a week in interest and to find a sum of NU 600 (including the week's interest) to get out of debt. The union pressed for and obtained strengthened legislation and more local enforcement of loan laws, but the money-lenders then became radio, television and household appliance salesmen, charging extremely high interest rates for credit purchases.

Project plan and method

The union already had several special projects servicing members' needs when it decided that the only way of countering the high cost of borrowing was a savings and loan scheme. It began an educational and publicity programme through its education department, in its newspaper and at meetings. Members were confident that the organisation would be able to manage such a scheme, as it had already demonstrated its abilities in other schemes. The union negotiated an arrangement with the employer whereby the savings authorised by the worker would be deducted from his weekly pay and transferred to the savings and loan scheme.

The minimum amount of weekly savings required to join the scheme was set at the fairly high level of NU 2 a week, which was over 5 per cent of the weekly income of the lowest-paid group; it was considered, however, that this group would in the main be borrowers rather than savers. The NU 2 minimum savings a week is only a little over 1 per cent of the weekly income of the highest-paid group, who would be the main savers.

The union donated not only its administrative capability to this project but also met, out of its general funds, the scheme's overhead costs of organisation, advice, guidance, equipment and office accommodation.

Over three-quarters of the members of the union have joined the savings scheme and are each saving a minimum of NU 2 a week. The scheme lends to union members over NU 2 million a year. These members have become savers for the first time in their lives and can plan ahead for their future. The borrowers are in an entirely new situation. The union member who now wants to borrow NU 200 does not have to take NU 300 more than he wants and can and does pay back his loan in instalments. Where formerly he paid as much as NU 100 a week (20 per cent a week on NU 500) for the NU 200 he needed, he now pays only NU 2 a month (1 per cent per month of unpaid balance) for the NU 200, and less as he pays back the loan.

From the very beginning this scheme has operated without any deficit.

Observations and conclusions

To be successful, savings and loan schemes require several things. While there is no lack of borrowers, a union cannot start such a scheme without first finding out, through research and investigations, the kinds of loan (amount and purpose) that are needed and the borrowers' ability to repay loans over a reasonable period of time. The number of savers among rural wage earners will depend on whether saving has been the custom. If the idea of saving is new, much educational and publicity work must be done before starting the scheme. Arranging with the employer to deduct the savings authorised by the worker from his pay greatly reduces the costs of the scheme. At least in the early stages, the scheme may have to limit in some way the frequency and amounts of the savers' withdrawals from their accounts. If all the savers were to withdraw all their savings on the same day, the scheme would be unworkable because much of the money would already be out on loan to members.

The scheme should grant loans only to members of the union. If the scheme so develops that more money is being saved than is being borrowed, it can place the surplus on deposit with a bank, which in turn will lend the money. However, the scheme would receive less interest on the money deposited with the bank, so that, if that situation continued, the scheme would eventually have to lower the rate of interest paid to members who save.

Any rural workers' organisation which feels that there is a definite need and possibility for such a savings and loan scheme within its membership should inquire from the national trade union centre whether any other union in the country has such a scheme and obtain technical help in evaluating the situation. If such help is not available, the organisation should contact its international trade secretariat, which can often interest international organisations of credit unions in providing research and technical assistance without charge.

Almost all existing savings and loan schemes operated by rural workers' organisations are for wage earners. Self-employed rural workers do not receive weekly or monthly incomes; their cash income comes once or twice a year except when they can obtain temporary or seasonal work as wage earners. Yet the self-employed are in need of loans for seeds, fertilisers, pesticides, and so on; however, they need such loans for only a few months until the sale of their products enables them to pay off the total loan. Some preliminary studies have been carried out on the possibility of making the savings of wage earners available as short-term loans to self-employed workers; but much remains to be done in this respect. One obvious way is through a workers' bank.

The possibilities of increasing the savings of all categories of worker in developing countries and investing them in job-creating industries within the country have in fact been receiving increasing attention on the part of unions and governments. One such instance was briefly touched on above under Case A (organisation of plantation workers), where, in addition to the savings and loan scheme, the union was putting additional savings from members into union-operated schemes to start new industries. In another organisation, the wages of many seasonal migrant workers are to be lent back on a seasonal basis to employers and the interest used to help to finance the union's welfare schemes.

Purchasing and marketing schemes

Background and special needs of members

Purchasing and marketing schemes are schemes of a co-operative type, run by peasant farmers in order to reduce the prices they pay for the materials and equipment they need to produce their crops, and in order to increase the prices they receive for their produce (thereby augmenting their income). These are two of the major interests of peasant farmers and, consequently, of a peasant organisation. There are several peasant organisations which have developed purchasing/marketing schemes as special services to members. Where the national law allows a co-operative to have a closed membership, it is normally the organisations which form and register purchasing and marketing co-operatives. As there are some countries which do not allow closed membership co-operatives, peasant organisations in those countries often develop other forms for this service to members by setting up "enterprises", or they provide the service informally as a project or scheme within the organisation.[1]

There are peasant organisations operating purchasing/marketing schemes both where an agrarian reform is under way and where no agrarian reform is taking place. Such schemes are needed by the members of the organisations in both cases, but an organisation can often utilise state resources to develop these services only when there is an existing agrarian reform activity.

Project plans and methods

It was shown under Case B how a national peasant federation was able to set up purchasing and marketing schemes in a developing country where an important agrarian reform was being carried out by government. Similarly, Case C illustrated how a new regional peasant union was able in a very short time to provide a variety of purchasing activities as a service to peasant and landless labourer members. The

---

[1] See also note to p. 12.

most important purchasing activity of that union may turn out to be related to the cottage industries which it has set up. As for the purchasing and marketing schemes of the rural workers' organisation described under Case E, one of their purposes was to increase the organisation's membership.[1]

Observations and conclusions

By reducing costs or raising prices received, the purchasing/marketing services of peasant unions—however they may be organised and registered and whatever they may be called—cater for the principal need of the members: an increase in income. Where little or no agrarian reform is taking place, the need for peasant organisations to perform this service is at its greatest; but, as was shown under Case B, the need is still present where there is active agrarian reform. The effect of the reform is, moreover, that the organisation is able to do much more of this type of servicing because some resources of government will be available to it.

Case C indicated how peasant unions can utilise purchasing/marketing services not only to increase the agricultural income of members but also as part of projects to provide employment opportunities for underemployed peasants, their unemployed families and landless labourers. Because they contribute to increasing peasant income, purchasing/marketing activities should be considered by more peasant unions as a way to increase their membership and to maintain the dues payments of their existing members.

A peasant union considering purchasing/marketing services to members will have to undertake a good deal of basic information collection and survey work. A fair amount of technical advice and assistance may also be necessary. Fortunately, the number of international and national organisations which will provide peasant unions with the kind of help they need for these activities is steadily increasing.

Consumer co-operative and similar schemes

The prices that rural workers pay for items of first necessity—the local staple food (rice, maize, other cereals), cooking oil, fuel, salt, spices, soap, and so on—account for a large proportion of their total cost of living. To cite an extreme case: the combined earnings, after deductions, of a husband and wife, both working on a tea plantation, with three children, amounted to NU 182.82 a month, of which NU 170.55, or 93 per cent, was spent on food alone.[2] Since reductions in the prices of

---

[1] For further information on these schemes, reference should be made to Cases B, C and E.

[2] ILO: *Housing, medical and welfare facilities and occupational safety and health on plantations,* Report III, Committee on Work on Plantations, Seventh Session, Geneva, 1976, p. 29.

first-necessity items have the effect of increasing real wages, an organisation of rural wage earners will be futhering and defending the interests of its members by endeavouring to secure such reductions.

Using traditional union methods, some rural workers' organisations have made representations to government in relation to price policies. In some countries laws have been enacted requiring employers of a minimum number of workers on plantations to establish employer-operated shops for basic necessities with controlled prices.

There are also rural wage earners' organisations which have used traditional collective bargaining methods by negotiating for employer shops operating at or below cost. However, there are also many rural workers' organisations which, being unable to further and defend the interest of their members in price reductions through representation or negotiation, develop co-operative schemes or activities designed to eliminate as many of the middlemen as possible.

Four selected cases [1]

Two examples of a rural workers' organisation engaging in consumer activities on behalf of its members have already been given. One of them is the national federation of peasant farmers (Case B), whose marketing enterprise also sells food and other items to the peasants at reduced prices. The other is the national federation of organisations of peasant farmers and plantation workers (Case E), which is planning to provide its members with consumer services. This federation already negotiates with employers regarding the type of goods to be sold in company stores and the prices to be charged, and has succeeded in some collective agreements in getting goods sold at less than cost prices.

To these two examples may be added two more. One of them is a large and strong national union of sugar workers, both field and factory. This union uses traditional methods of negotiation to obtain from the employers facilities and finance for consumer co-operatives and union consumer shops but also uses special services to bring about the establishment of the co-operatives and shops.

The other organisation is a strong rural wage earners' union which has engaged in special services to meet the members' consumer needs for both first-necessity and many other items.

The large and strong union of sugar workers has, as a part of its national trade union centre, represented the consumer interests of its members with the national government in the case of policies for controlling or subsidising the prices of basic necessities. In negotiations with the employers' federation, this rural workers' organisation has obtained

---

[1] For the purposes of this section of the book, it will be convenient to consider simultaneously the topics that are examined separately in other sections under "Background", "Special needs of members" and "Project plans and methods".

acceptance of the following conditions in a collective agreement: that no employer can be associated, whether directly or indirectly, with any shop on his estate or near his estate which sells articles of first necessity; that, if the estate is situated at a distance of more than 5 kilometres from an established public market, the employer must set aside land and erect stalls for a free public market next to the workers' housing; that, if the workers on the estate form a consumer co-operative or a union store, the employer is obliged to lend money of a specified amount depending on the quantity of his annual sugar production to assist in starting up the co-operative or union store and also to provide it with office accommodation free of charge. Under such conditions the union has to provide only technical guidance and assistance to those of its local units which want to establish union consumer shops. The union has also encouraged a national consumer co-operative organisation to establish consumer co-operatives at the local level.

Our final example, the strong rural wage earners' organisation, was unable to obtain, through its representations, any government price policy, and consequently started special services to meet the consumer needs of its members. At first, the union intended to organise and register consumer co-operatives for its members, but the national law required that co-operatives must be open to all, not only to union members. The union's attitude was that, if its resources (finance, personnel and facilities) were to be used, it could justify the project only if it furthered and defended the interest of members alone. Accordingly, stores and services were organised without open membership, but on what was in effect a co-operative basis.

This union eventually established four stores from which lorries also go out with goods to the housing areas on the plantations. As in all cases of consumer activities by rural workers' organisations, the merchants were forced to lower their prices to meet union competition. For example, the prices of sugar, rice and beans were reduced by, respectively, about 17 per cent, 18 per cent and 20 per cent. These price reductions increased substantially the purchasing power of that proportion of the members' wages which was available for expenditure on necessities sold under the union's scheme.

As in co-operatives, the union sold shares in the consumer scheme to members wishing to buy them. In addition to the savings already noted, union members who are not shareholders receive a 1.5 per cent further reduction in prices and the union scheme pays the 3 per cent government purchase tax, making an additional saving of 4.5 per cent. The union member who is a shareholder in the union scheme receives this 4.5 per cent plus an additional 4 per cent, thus reducing the cost of his purchases by 8.5 per cent. With the experience gained over time, the union has greatly increased the variety of items offered for sale to members.

The national federation of organisations of wage earners and peasants (Case E) operates under a law which requires an employer to set up an employer-run store on any plantation which has 25 or more workers. This requirement was itself partly the result of representations to government by the national trade union centre. The federation also uses two traditional methods to make this law effective. One of them is inspection to see that all provisions of the law are applied and, if not, to report the infringements to government. The second method consists in negotiations with employers to obtain better conditions than the law requires of them. As this rural workers' federation is not yet strong enough to force the employers to negotiate as a single employers' federation, it has to negotiate with each employer separately. The best collective agreement negotiated so far with respect to consumer affairs requires the employer to sell to the workers a specified list of goods which he has purchased wholesale at the nearest large seaport (not the nearest town, where the purchase prices would be higher) and to sell the goods at cost price to the workers, the employer paying all costs of transport of the goods and all other costs, including the wages of the workers in the shop.

In addition, and as was noted under Case E, this federation is starting a special service for its peasant members which combines the marketing of their produce with the supply of first-necessity items to the peasants and of other goods to the wage-earning members.

As for the large and strong national federation of peasant farmers (Case B), while it is not able to cater for the consumer needs of its peasant members by negotiation, it can and does cater for them through representations to government—both directly and in conjunction with the national trade union centre to which it is affiliated. In addition, and as was noted under Case B, it has established special consumer service activities tied to the pick-up stations of its marketing activities, so that, when the peasant member brings his produce to these stations, he has the opportunity to buy basic consumer items and some basic production requisites such as fertiliser, seed and simple agricultural implements.

Observations and conclusions

The case of the national union of sugar workers provides a classic illustration of a workers' organisation defending the interests of its members by attacking their problem on all fronts: representation, negotiation, mixed negotiation and special services (loans and facilities negotiated from the employers, but shops run by co-operatives or by the union itself); encouraging others to operate the special services (through a strong national consumer co-operative organisation); and operating the consumer service only where needed or wanted by the local units; and even then providing only the technical advice and assistance needed by

Development of village crafts as alternative occupations in Colombia (above)

Good milk cattle provide improved diet and additional income in Kenya (below)

the local officers. The activities of this union again emphasise that a rural workers' organisation should provide a special service only when and in so far as there is no other way of meeting a particular need of the membership.

It is, however, worth noting that, both among rural and among other workers' organisations, there appears to be a high rate of failure in their consumer schemes and sponsored co-operatives. A full explanation of all the various causes of these failures would call for far more information than is available; but, on the basis of such information as is available, the following points may be made.

1. Consumer services may appear, at first sight, to be relatively easy to operate: the officers and members of an organisation see that people with the same level of education as themselves are running small family shops. The many failures make it plain, however, that this first impression is mistaken: the fact is that operating a consumer service on a scale suited to a plantation or an industrial enterprise is an undertaking that requires a considerable amount of managerial ability and experience—perhaps even more than for any other special service described in this book.

2. The apparent ease of running a consumer service may tempt a rural workers' organisation to engage in that activity without having collected sufficient information on questions such as wholesale costs, transport costs, overhead costs, wage costs, local sellers' mark-ups of each item, exact consumer needs of the members and their interest in consumer services, possibility of meeting the needs otherwise than by means of a special service, and so on.

3. A rural workers' organisation may make the serious mistake of failing to seek and obtain the technical advice and assistance that is available. The possible sources of assistance may include the national trade union centre (though caution is required if its experience is exclusively urban), national co-operative organisations, government and rural workers' international trade secretariats.

It appears from the information available that the rural workers' organisations which have been most successful in providing consumer services for rural wage earners fall into one or the other of two categories. On the one hand, there is the strong rural workers' organisation which can obtain some of what is needed for this special service through negotiation with employers and which can provide managerial skills gained in other activities. On the other hand, there is the enterprise union or local unit of a national organisation established on a very isolated plantation. While certain organisations of this second type have operated a co-operative activity for some years, it should be noted that they have limited the items sold to a very small number of basic necessities. This limitation

Simple irrigation systems such as this example
in Chad increase peasants' production and income

appears to be highly desirable throughout a prolonged initial stage of the service.

Even less information is available on the consumer services of peasant unions, whose activities in this field have hitherto probably been much less extensive than those of organisations of rural wage earners. The cases that have been mentioned suggest the desirability of coupling consumer activities with marketing activities. Indeed, given the geographical dispersion of the peasant membership and the need to transport goods over great distances, the pairing of these activities would appear to be essential.

Yet, despite the pitfalls and the failures, there have been success stories. That there is much more that could and should be done by many rural workers' organisations in the provision of consumer services can be illustrated by reference to actual cases. There are sugar plantations where the workers have to buy basic commodities such as rice, milk, salt, dried fish, canned goods and clothing from shops run by the overseer or farm manager at prices that are from 25 to 60 per cent higher than those charged in stores in the town. Moreover, on some of these plantations the workers are compelled to buy from these stores as a condition of employment.[1] Ample sources of technical assistance and advice on methods of defeating this kind of exploitation are now obtainable by rural workers' organisations.

Housing schemes

Background

In developing countries, rural wage earners' housing is generally part of the plantation, estate or *hacienda*,[2] and the rural workers' unions further and defend their members' interests by negotiations with the employer for improved housing and by representations to the government for minimum standards in employer-provided housing.

In some cases, however, a rural workers' organisation develops a housing project of its own as a direct service to its members. Such cases usually fall into one or the other of two categories, both of which will be illustrated in this section from two organisations operating in the same country so that useful comparisons can be made.

The first organisation is the strong rural wage earners' union which was considered in the section on "Savings and loan schemes". To recapitulate the description of that union, its membership of some 12,000 wage earners includes both plantation workers producing field crops and

---

[1] ILO: *Housing, medical and welfare facilities . . .*, op. cit., p. 32.
[2] A large estate in Latin American countries.

some factory and technical workers engaged in processing and transporting the produce. This mixed composition of the membership is reflected in the wide difference in average income between the lowest-paid group (NU 150 a month) and the highest-paid group (over NU 600 a month). Membership dues are at the flat rate of NU 3.20 a month, which is equivalent to just over 2 per cent of the average income of the lowest-paid group. Over the years, this union, which has been in existence for over 20 years, has been able to raise the real wages of all members (generally to a greater degree for the lowest than for the highest paid), with the result that those in the middle and upper wage groups have been considering the possibility of housing away from the plantations.

The other organisation is a union of about 2,000 sharecroppers, tenants and small owner-occupiers. The membership dues are at the flat rate of NU 1 a month, which is probably equivalent to 2 per cent of the average income of the lowest-paid group (estimated here at about one-third of the average income of the lowest-paid members of the wage earners' union). Despite its small size, this peasant union has been able to accomplish a great deal for the benefit of its members. However, its particular relevance to the question of housing is that it had to cope with a natural disaster.

Special needs of members

The rural wage earners' union

As the members' income increased through the union's negotiations with the employer, many of them wanted to move themselves and their families out of the "barrack" type of housing common to many plantations and to have their own homes. In the company housing, six families live in one building with doorless rooms measuring 16 by 12 feet. There is no privacy. As the family grows, older children have to leave to make room for the rest. Since it is not his home, the worker has no incentive for improving his living quarters; it is just a place where everybody sleeps. The worker has merely to comply with the company regulations, which tell him when to clean, on what day he must put out the rubbish and that he must not play the radio at certain times.

The peasant union

Although self-employed rural workers, like rural wage earners, have housing problems, they too must wait for an increased income before they can attend to them. There are other interests to be furthered before the union can tackle housing. The membership of this union included, however, a community of 20 small owner-occupiers which suffered the disaster of a flood. Immediate help was needed, but, as all available assets of these rural workers had been used up in establishing the community, they did not have enough resources to rebuild their houses.

Project plans and methods

The rural wage earners' union

The union carried out much basic research, consulted many housing and construction technicians, looked for sources of loans and examined the members' ability to pay for housing. With a master plan for 184 houses, the union started a union housing co-operative department. Having obtained, on the evidence of its demonstrated capacity in earlier projects, a loan from an international development agency, the union built the 184 houses. Each house has an area of 76 square metres, consists of three bedrooms, a living-room, a kitchen, a dining-room and a bathroom and stands on a plot of land of 300 square metres. The cost to each member buying a house was NU 4,100, with an interest charge on any unpaid balance at the rate of 6 per cent a year.

This project was carried out by combining the assets of the union and of the union co-operatives. The union negotiated a clause in a collective agreement whereby it would receive from the company, for its union housing scheme, the necessary land and also part of the cost of preparing the land for housing. The cost of surveying, planning and administration was borne by the union. Had only a co-operative approach been used, each house would have cost very much more. It was by combining the strength and negotiating power of a union with the co-operative approach that it was possible to provide houses at a price within reach of the 184 members who bought them.

Pursuing its housing scheme, the union subsequently obtained from the plantation company a substantial grant which enabled it to build 1,200 houses and to sell them to its members at prices ranging, according to the size and model of the house, from NU 3,000 to NU 4,800. Moreover, the purchasers were able to raise loans with an interest charge at the rate of 6 per cent a year and payable over a period of 10 to 24 years. A member who, for example, obtained a maximum loan for one of the cheaper houses would become the owner of a house of his own in less than 20 years by redeeming the loan and the interest charge with a monthly payment of NU 25. This would be equivalent to 17 per cent of the income of the lowest-paid plantation workers.

The peasant union

The peasant union appealed to its international trade secretariat for a grant of NU 25,000. The secretariat was able to raise this amount through assistance from another affiliate. The 20 houses were built with a cement-block foundation, wood-frame walls and zinc-sheet roofing.

The houses are much larger and of much better construction than the original houses. Since they were built on the same land, there were no land costs and the grant was sufficient to build 20 houses at a cost of NU 1,250 each.

Observations and conclusions

The case of the rural wage earners' union again illustrates how an organisation recognised by employer and government as the voice of rural workers will receive attention and obtain assistance in solving the special problems of its members. Moreover, where such a union has previously demonstrated its ability to develop and operate special projects servicing the special needs of members, it can even obtain (as in this case) loans and grants that will enable it to build houses to be owned by its members at a total cost amounting (it is estimated in this case) to over NU 10 million.

But perhaps the most important observation that may be made on this case is that it shows how much can be accomplished through the strength and negotiating power of a wage earners' union (or the pressure power of a peasant union), when combined with the co-operative approach. The results in this case could not have been achieved by the co-operative approach alone, necessary though that approach also generally is for housing services, as well as for many other types of service.

The case of the peasant union was a case of charity. The leaders of peasant unions strongly condemn charity as a solution to the problems of peasants in developing countries. They consider that charity in fact holds back solutions and reforms. They recognise, however, that natural disasters call for exceptional treatment and that all victims of floods, hurricanes, earthquakes and other natural disasters need help. Yet even an adversity of this kind can be turned to advantage. In this case the union could have started a special housing or disaster scheme of its own. With the permission of the donors, which would have been given, it could have used the sum of NU 25,000 to make to each of these members a grant of NU 1,000 and an interest-free loan of NU 250 to be repaid over five or even ten years. In that way a fund would have become available in due course for other schemes. For example, by buying materials in quantity and with members themselves doing the work during the non-agricultural season, the cost of these houses could be halved. With the money from the repayment of the loans plus some assistance from other organisations, this peasant union could considerably improve the housing of many of its small owner-occupier members.

Community development

Background

By "community development" is meant local projects which meet local needs and which, in developed countries, would be considered the responsibility of local government—drinking-water, a road to the next village, a bridge, a school house, a social centre, a medical clinic. Community development activities in developing countries do exist without the participation of trade unionism and, when community development is sponsored and promoted over a wide area by organisations which are not workers' organisations, such community development activities may be an impediment to the formation of peasant unions. Some local need or needs are met and thus some of the motivation for the peasants to form or join unions may be lacking.

Community development as understood here will refer to services which are fostered by, and, in large measure, run under the guidance of, the local unit of a peasant federation or union.

The first rural workers' organisation to be considered is a national federation of mainly peasant members. It operates in a country where not much agrarian reform of any importance is taking place but where there are some virgin lands belonging to the national government. From time to time, some of this land is opened up for settlement. When this happens, the national federation assists members who want to migrate in order to acquire land.

A second organisation is a national peasant federation, some of whose local units consist of primitive communities from which workers go out to till the land of others.

A third case concerns sharecroppers, tenants and small farmers. A few leaders who had organised community development activities in their own communities realised that many of their most serious problems could be solved only at the national level. They tried to form a national peasant federation and to register it under the national labour laws but found that the law expressly prohibited this. Instead, they formed "community development unions" on a provincial basis. These helped to form base units. Others followed suit and soon there were such organisations in several provinces. Eventually, the provincial organisations came together and formed a national "communal union".[1]

---

[1] Whatever may be the name for it (association, organisation, federation, union, communal union, indigenous league, league of communities, etc.), any organisation whose membership is confined to workers and whose function is to further and defend the economic, social and other interests of its members is a workers' union.

Special needs of members

As already noted, community development covers all those common local services which, in developed countries, are regarded as the responsibility of local authorities or of central government. In the case of the first organisation, since this is a community to be started from scratch in virgin territory, it will need everything, beginning with housing. A first community need will be for water for drinking, cooking and washing and for the livestock. The satisfaction of other needs will be a matter of setting priorities. As for the needs of the primitive communities in the second case, they are often as great and as varied as in the first case, although the motivation of a "fresh start" is absent. In the third case, the special needs were for savings and loan schemes, multiple co-operatives and legal representation on land matters.

Project plans and methods

The main functions of the first rural workers' organisation at the national level have been to supply any necessary technical advice and planning based on experience gained over time with community development activities. In the second and third cases, the national federations have also been largely responsible for arousing interest in community development activities through information and education programmes aimed at suitable base units. So far as the third case in particular is concerned, by coupling a well thought out community development programme with co-operative activities for the development of local units throughout the country, the union became a truly national organisation of rural workers within less than ten years.

In all these cases it is the local units of the rural workers' organisations which, owing to the nature of the activities, have been responsible for the projects. While these projects are designed to serve the whole of the local community, including persons who may not be members of the rural workers' organisation, it was the officers of the peasant unions who, in all three cases, provided the leadership and the administration.

In so far as money was needed to buy materials that could not be made locally, it was (as is normal in these cases) raised within the community, usually on the basis of ability to pay. The ability to pay of all the members of a union is well known in these small, closed communities. Contributions in labour are also required and are in fact the greatest input of the majority of community development projects.

Observations and conclusions

Community development projects have proved to be a very important special service of rural workers' organisations: they could and should be used more widely. They help to meet needs of rural workers even in countries where an agrarian reform is under way, because these countries will not have sufficient resources to meet all of the needs in every community. Furthermore, a community development project carried out by the local unit of a national peasant union demonstrates the value of the union to other local units and to rural workers generally.

Community development activities enable a national peasant organisation to accomplish a great deal throughout the country with a very small expenditure. All that is needed is the development of a limited technical ability and of an information and education programme to foster and guide such activities when undertaken for the first time by a local unit. Furthermore, those national peasant unions which have demonstrated their ability to advise and guide local units in such projects can obtain technical and financial help from other organisations for the technically more difficult projects (such as bridge construction). In fact, some international development agencies will cover one-half of the costs of more complicated community development projects and count the donated labour of union members as part of the other half.

When community development projects are undertaken during the non-agricultural season, they enable underemployed union members to take part in the solution of some of their local social and economic problems.

National and international rural workers' organisations now include the subject of community development projects in their education programmes for local and national leaders. Useful though this work is, it is not enough. There is a need to prepare for each country specific and detailed case studies showing what has been done, what remains to be done and what help is available from the national organisation.

Technical agrarian services

The technical agrarian services to be considered here consist in the information, advice and assistance on technical matters with which a peasant union provides its members for the purpose of enabling them either to increase their income or to reduce their losses. While the advice and information must be, of course, such that the peasant member can afford to apply it, technical agrarian services can be of great value to the members, especially in countries where no agrarian reform of any importance is taking place.

What the members of peasant unions need is to increase their production, and hence their income, with very little (if any) outlay of cash. In the section on Case C concerning a local organisation of sharecroppers, tenant farmers, small owner-occupiers and landless day labourers, a number of examples were given of technical agrarian services designed to increase the income of very poor peasants and even of landless labourers.

The key to the provision of technical agrarian services to the members of a peasant union lies with the field representative. Any effective rural workers' organisation of some size will have one or more field representatives who visit each base unit regularly and, in addition, any unit faced with a problem or emergency. Depending on the country and the organisation, these field representatives are referred to as organisers or organiser/educators or activists or representatives or business agents. They are full-time paid officials and are usually appointed by the national or federation executive committee. Although there is seldom any provision for them in the constitution of a union, they play a crucial role in the successful development, operation and administration of a workers' organisation. They are expected to be specialists in many fields: organisers, educators, advocates, administrators, negotiators, conciliators. They represent and are at the service of, on the one hand, the local members and their base organisation and, on the other, the executive committee.

Where an organisation of rural workers is not yet sufficiently strong in numbers and financial resources to employ field representatives, it falls to the full-time officials on the executive committee to perform these functions when an emergency arises. It is not easy, however, for these officials to spare any of the time that they have to devote to their own important national duties. In any case, the union members at the base units need the services of field representatives not only in emergencies but regularly.[1] Field representatives can be and are in fact being trained to serve also as technical agrarian advisers. As was noted in the case of the local organisation of sharecroppers, tenant farmers, small owner-occupiers and landless day labourers (Case C), the field representatives were sent to a variety of specialised government and private institutions to study such technical agrarian subjects as soil testing, fertilisers, irrigation, household dairying, domestic poultry keeping and fish production. The field representatives then assisted the organisation's members by giving them technical advice and information on the way to start new practices and even new methods of raising their incomes. That peasant union deliberately concentrated on those activities, such as fish production, domestic poultry keeping and household dairying, for which government and private assistance is available. In all cases, the union provided only technical advice that at least some of the members would be economically able to apply, and in fact most of the advice given was of a kind which the members could apply.

The provision of technical agrarian services can often be successfully undertaken by any federation whose members need and want it, so long as it has its own field representatives. These representatives can be sent to various institutes and schools for training at little or no cost. They can

---

[1] This information relating to field representatives is taken from ILO: *Structure and functions of workers' organisations,* op. cit.

even be trained in simple or basic veterinarian services for the prevention, recognition and treatment of animal diseases. They can keep abreast of the findings of experiments at model farms and select from the findings the information worth passing on to members. Every kind of agricultural development programme which may be instituted and which grants benefits to peasants can be quickly and easily made known to members, and the field representatives can assist in processing any necessary paper work.

Technical agrarian services provided by rural workers' organisations are very similar to their education or health care schemes in that they are providing services which, in developed countries, are normally performed by the ministry of agriculture and agricultural extension services. Where an organisation is unable to obtain this service for members from government through representation, it provides it through its own activities. Organisations which add the provision of technical agrarian services to the functions of field representatives may well discover that they are recruiting new members who also want to obtain those services −another case of special services acting also as an organising tool. It should be the first priority of any peasant organisation, before undertaking to provide any technical agrarian services, to equip itself with field representatives and then to give them the appropriate technical agrarian training.

A peasant organisation may be able to further and defend some of the interests of its membership as a whole without having full-time paid field representatives; but it is only with the help of field representatives who visit the base units both regularly and in response to emergencies that it can further and defend the interests not only of the membership as a whole but also of the individual members. Peasants, like all workers, will all the more readily join a union and support it financially if it looks after their individual as well as their collective needs.

Technical agrarian services, while probably using up less of the resources of a peasant organisation than any other special service, can further the individual member's central interest, which is to increase his income.

Educational services

Background and special needs of members

The provision of education (with the exception of workers' education) is another service to rural workers which, in developed countries, is normally regarded as the responsibility of government; but, depending on the resources available and the government's priorities, rural workers and their families in developing countries may have certain educational needs that are not being met. Taking only the case of basic education for the children of rural workers in developing countries, it has been pointed out that "for 300 million children of poor farmers ... there are still no schools—and for hundreds of millions of others if a school, no qualified teacher—and if a qualified teacher, no adequate books".[1]

There are, moreover, other educational needs too—vocational training and higher education for young people; vocational retraining for unemployed adults; simple agrarian technical education for peasants; adult literacy training; and health, nutrition and family planning education. While the needs in all these cases are on a staggeringly large scale, the resources available are limited. There are, however, many rural workers' organisations which are providing their members and their families with various special educational services.

Project plans and methods

Rural wage earners

One of the organisations of rural wage earners which has done much to meet some of the educational needs of its members and their families is the "enterprise" union of 12,000 plantation workers which was discussed in the section on "Savings and loan schemes". As was noted in that section, one of the six departments of the union's co-operative plan is for education. The union has spent as much as 23 per cent of its annual income on education. Some of this expenditure is for workers' education, but most of it is for special educational services. Under the national law, plantation employers are required to provide education for the children of workers only for the first three years of schooling. Under its own education programme, the union called meetings of interested members who were fathers of children and developed a basic plan. It negotiated with the employer for the necessary buildings on the various plantations. Working with the ministry of education, the union sponsored a programme for 14 schools providing the first six years of education. The union next looked at the schools for secondary education in the area and found that they were run as highly commercialised ventures, charging high fees and employing only trainee teachers (at low salaries) and undergraduates, among whom the teachers of accounting, for example, did not know how to make even a simple entry in a ledger. Under its educational scheme, the union took over a secondary school in financial difficulties, employed only fully qualified teachers and reduced the fees to about 70 per cent of the previous rates. It added a full physics and chemistry laboratory to the school. The school enrolled over 1,000 pupils. In order to compete with the union's school, the quality of the

---

[1] Robert S. McNamara: *Address to the Board of Governors* (Washington, DC, World Bank, 25 Sep. 1972).

other schools in the area has been improved, to the benefit of the whole community. In the case of members having two or more children in the school, the union pays the fees for one of them. Members receiving the lowest wages pay only half the full fee for their children.

The union has added to this secondary school an extension which offers vocational training in mechanics, welding, carpentry and electronics. Pupils in the secondary school who wish to go on to a university are encouraged to take basic vocational courses so that they may obtain employment to support themselves during their university studies.

Acting in conjunction with the government, the union operates a large literacy programme for members and their adult families. The need and value of such literacy training became clear to the union when it first established its savings and loan scheme, because the money-lenders opposing the scheme falsely depicted it as a union scheme for robbing the members. In its literacy training programmes the union was able to adapt traditional material to the particular interests and experiences of the various groups within its membership, thereby reversing earlier failures in the programme. Several thousand members and their adult families have already been taught to read and write through this scheme.

This union's education programme also includes lectures and seminars on family planning and family education.

Some reference was made under Case A to the special educational services of a very strong and large national union of plantation workers. The services include a vocational training institute established in conjunction with government and an international vocational education foundation which trains unemployed plantation workers and children of members in those technical skills needed for the union's own enterprises and for new industries being established by public and private undertakings; a family planning education programme; a system of scholarships and study loans for the higher education of members' children; two hostels in the university city to provide accommodation at the lowest possible cost for students who are children of members; an adult literacy programme which is lowering the rate of illiteracy among the members and their families; and a project for a library on every estate.

Apart from these two examples of unions which are offering a wide variety of educational services to their members and their families, there are many other rural workers' organisations which provide at least some of the services referred to above.

Peasants

The needs of peasant farmers for various educational services are even greater than those of rural wage earners, if only because there are many times more peasants than wage earners in the rural sectors of developing countries. In many areas the main work of providing primary education has been undertaken by peasant federations as part of their community development services (described in an earlier section). Where government can assign teachers but does not have sufficient resources to build the school, community building projects have been sponsored by the base units of peasant federations, using the labour of the community and cash contributions from all members of the community, the amount of these being based on ability to pay. Many peasant unions, working in conjunction with government or institutions, are providing health, nutrition and family courses and adult literacy training. In countries where an important agrarian reform is taking place and where, consequently, the rural sector receives priority consideration in the allocation of resources, peasant federations are in a better position to obtain educational facilities and services of all types for their members and families through representation and pressure-group activities.

The local organisation of sharecroppers, tenant farmers, small owner-occupiers and landless day labourers described under Case C provides an example of a peasant union operating in a country where little agrarian reform is taking place and whose members are greatly in need of many educational services. For example, 71 per cent of the men and 96 per cent of the women in the area served by this union are illiterate. This union has, however, concentrated first on the members' most pressing need, which is for an increased income. Its policy has been to provide "education by action" (functional education) and it has in fact provided much education—mainly vocational training—by this method in only one year.[1]

Observations and conclusions

There is a very grave shortage of educational services of all types in the rural sectors of most developing countries. Working in conjunction with governments and other institutions, rural workers' organisations are doing a great deal to relieve the shortage. Wage earners' unions and peasant federations are, moreover, being encouraged by various international institutes to provide educational services, particularly adult literacy training. The difficulty is that rural workers often give a very low priority to literacy training. Unions have to determine with care and on the basis of detailed surveys whether the members want this service and will use it. Even when another organisation wants to support this service and is willing to provide most of the resources, the programme still requires some of the valuable time of the union leadership; and if it fails, either because of lack of interest on the part of the members or because it was badly planned and operated by others, it may weaken the union.

---

[1] See under Case C the particulars of the union's special services relating to training in household dairying, woollen blanket manufacturing, sewing, fish farming, and so on, as well as in preventive medicine and health care.

Technical and vocational training to increase the production of peasant farmers and to provide alternative types of employment for wage earners are more likely to be given a high priority by the members, and increasing numbers of international institutes are ready to support these educational special services.

Health care schemes

Background

Workers' organisations in developed countries generally further and defend the interests of members in health care for themselves and their families by representation and pressure-group activities. Some unions also negotiate private insurance cover for the cost of private medical care. Rural workers' organisations, particularly those in developing countries, are often faced with the fact that governments with very limited resources may not give high priority to rural health care.

A very few rural workers' organisations have turned to special services as a means of meeting their members' need for health care, but much more remains to be done and could be done in many countries. In the case of the organisation of seasonal agricultural workers (Case D), a health care scheme was not only its principal special service but was one of the workers' main reasons for forming and joining the union. It was, however, noted that the case itself was the special one of a large and isolated concentration of migrant workers without their families, with a very high incidence of sickness and mortality yet without any local health care facilities whatsoever.

A wider range of situations will be considered in this section on health care for rural workers, both wage earners and peasants.

Special needs of members

Rural wage earners

Unions of rural wage earners in developing countries have been able to obtain some health care for members and their families through representation and pressure-group activities with government and by negotiation with employers. Despite a dearth of statistics, the information available suggests that health care available to rural wage earners and their families is generally provided by the employer in the case of the larger enterprises (plantations, estates, and so on). Plantations employing more than a specified minimum number of workers are in fact often required by law to provide them with health care. The quality and the range of this type of health care vary very widely with the enterprise. On most of the smaller plantations the employer does not provide any health care.

Where the law requires the employer to provide health care, the first task of the unions is to verify that any stipulations relating to the quality and quantity of care to be provided are being applied. Unions then try to bring the health care of their members into the sphere of collective bargaining, with a view to raising both its quality and quantity, and to negotiate for union representation in its planning and administration. There are two possible ways of improving health care on plantations where it is furnished by the employer. One is for the government to subsidise the employer's improvements of his health services; the other is to make health care improvement the first priority in the next round of wage or other negotiations with the employer. The second method raises, however, the question of the members' own views of their interests. Very often, the worst forms of health care, as well as of housing, provided by employers on plantations are to be found in extremely poor countries—so poor, to quote one example, that a man and his wife, both working 25 days a month, may earn only just enough to feed themselves and three children. If either of them misses work because of illness or if there are more than three children to feed, the family will not have enough food.[1] In that kind of situation, no member of a union is going to vote to give improved health care priority over an increase in wages; but the inadequacy of the employer's provision of health care will be liable to find expression in a go-slow or stoppage of work.

For workers on small plantations where no health care is provided by the employer, their best hope lies in coming together as members of a centralised national union which can both represent their interests at the national level and inquire into the possibility of setting up a special union health care service.

Peasants

Even less information is available on existing health care provided for peasants and their families. Since the question of a legal obligation on large employers to provide health care does not arise in the case of peasants, the provision of health care depends largely on government priorities and resources. The first line of attack is clearly representation and pressure-group activities by a strong national peasant federation. There are very few cases of peasant unions providing health care as a special service.

---

[1] ILO: *Housing, medical and welfare facilities . . .*, op. cit., p. 29.

Project plans and methods

Rural wage earners

For plantation workers (generally those on small plantations) for whom the employer does not provide any health care, a centralised national union may be able to provide facilities on a regional basis as a special service to members and their families. In an area containing enough small plantations, the economics of providing the area as a whole with health care services may be worth investigating. The process of investigation would be very similar to the surveys carried out by the organisation of seasonal agricultural workers described under Case D. The economic problem, however, would be much more difficult to solve because (unlike Case D, where there were no non-working wives and children to consider) there would be non-working wives, children and possibly older dependants to be taken into account on many, if not most, of the small plantations. For each contributor to a health care scheme, there would be several potential users. Assuming that the members could and would contribute to a union health care scheme, each contribution might have to cover an average of four or five persons instead of only one person under Case D. However, where there is no health care whatever on a small plantation, union members might be willing to pay for at least some care, however thinly spread. Thus it might be possible to provide periodic visits by qualified medical personnel and some kind of system of transport for emergency cases. The employer himself might be persuaded, through negotiations, to make some contribution for each worker and each dependant. A union health care scheme would be, of course, out of the question if the union were not strong enough to obtain an employer's contribution in negotiations and if the members were not sufficiently interested to contribute to it.

Even if the potential contributions from members and from the employers seemed likely to be large enough to warrant further investigation, there would still be the question—often a critical one—of the availability of trained medical personnel willing and able to work in rural areas at salaries that a union health care scheme could afford to pay. For the rural areas of developing countries the services of fully qualified doctors would be, of course, unobtainable. The union would have to rely on dressers, paramedical staff, male nurses and similar trained medical personnel. There are various grades of training and skill. In some countries such personnel are trained in considerable and growing numbers in government public health institutes. In other countries the only available medical personnel are retired or former military orderlies, whose training may be only in first aid. It must be expected, therefore, that an organisation of rural wage earners could not hope to set up a health care scheme except in countries where well qualified medical technicians are being trained by the government in fairly large numbers;

*Literacy training provides
increased opportunities in Mali (above)*

Health care services in Turkey (below)

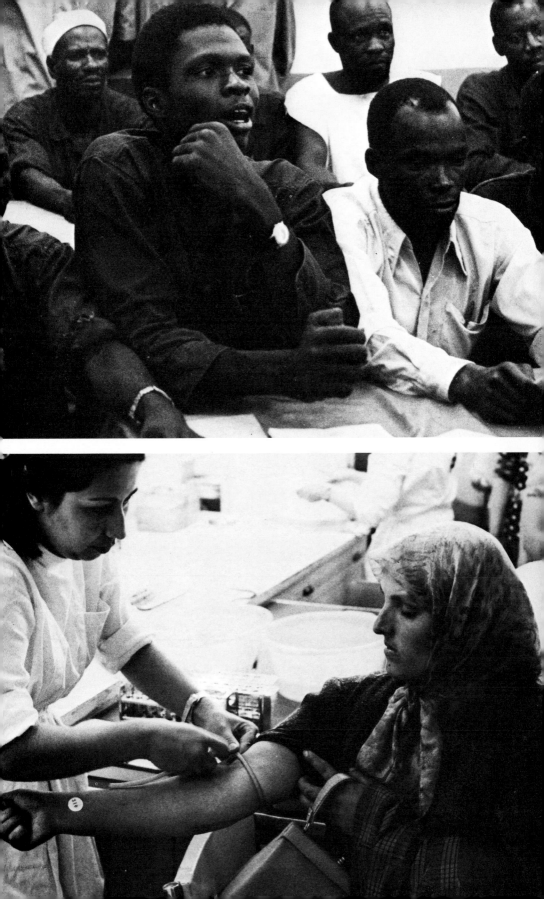

but, even in such countries, the organisation might have to offer high salaries in order to attract such staff to isolated rural areas.

Should the results of a union's preliminary investigations point to a probable sufficiency of income from members' contributions and to an adequate availability of suitably qualified medical personnel, the union's next step will be to seek help from others. It will need money for capital equipment, such as medical vans, and it will need the advice of an experienced organisation in planning its health care scheme so as to avoid making unnecessary and costly mistakes. For this advice, the union can best turn to the national centre and/or the international trade secretariat.

So far as health care provided by employers of rural wage earners is concerned, if it cannot be improved by negotiation with the employers and/or government subsidies, it will be for the union members to decide whether it is so poor that they would prefer to do without it and to contribute to a scheme of their own.[1]

Peasants

Unlike rural wage earners, peasant farmers have no employer with whom health care or a contribution to health care can be negotiated. Moreover, as they are likely to be geographically more scattered than wage earners, any health care scheme for them could be comparatively costly. A peasant union is limited to the traditional methods of representation and pressure-group activities in furthering the health care interests of its members and their families, but its success will depend not only on its own strength and ability but also on the resources and priorities of government.

Little has hitherto been done by peasant unions towards providing health care as a special service. One national peasant union is known to be concerned in a health care programme; however, this programme is based to only a small extent on a union special service, being dependent mainly on what is, in effect, charity. This union contributes some administration and organisation to a programme under which qualified medical practitioners regularly visit different areas. The medicines are donated by the international foundation which worked out the programme for the union, and the doctors make only a token charge for each visit, whether to union members or to peasants who are not members.

---

[1] There is a recorded case of a strong national union of agricultural wage earners, one-half of whose members covered by the collective agreement are migrant workers with families, which, because it operates in the rural sector of a developed country, has been able to replace health care provided by the employer (except for first-aid treatment of accidents on the job) by a health care scheme of its own. This has been possible because enough doctors are available for the union to engage them on a full-time basis. Moreover, excellent health facilities for specialised needs are available not too far from the rural area and are accessible over all-weather roads. Furthermore, the union has negotiated an employer contribution to the scheme in lieu of the employer health care.

Children of working mothers in a child care centre in Malaysia (above)   65

Providing a service to peasants in Bolivia
by registering their title to land (below)

It would be difficult for this union to operate a true union health care service—one that was "of, for and by" the members—because the country has no trained medical personnel other than qualified doctors, who, in any case, are in short supply and will decline to live in rural areas and whose fees would be far beyond the means of a peasant (for example, the fee for attending an uncomplicated birth would cost the peasant four years of income). It seems, therefore, that the only recourse for this national peasant federation would be to urge the government, through representations and pressure-group activities, to establish a public health institute for the training of medical technicians.

Where trained medical technicians can be engaged, a peasant federation may be able to operate union health care schemes. The process will be more or less the same as for unions of rural wage earners with memberships covering a number of small plantations. The peasant union may find that there are one or two regions in the country where the number of interested members living within a compact geographical area is sufficient to make it economically feasible to introduce a mobile medical van service, for example. If that service proves successful, the peasant union may then be able to operate a transport service for emergency cases.

Thus, even such little information as is available does suggest that some peasant federations could provide health care schemes as a special service for their members.

Observations and conclusions

In the highly developed countries more and more medical technicians are receiving some of the advanced training formerly confined to fully qualified medical practice. There is a special need for such technicians in developing countries. Where they are available, it becomes possible for unions of rural workers, whether of peasants or of wage earners, to run their own medical care schemes in the absence of government schemes. Medical schemes are not in fact as difficult to administer and operate as they might seem to be—probably they are less difficult to run than several other special services discussed in this book. The medical technicians engaged by the union carry out the technical work, leaving the union itself with the task of determining the quality and quantity of the health care which it can afford and of putting the quantity into effect. It is the government which, whether by law or upon request, will inspect and evaluate the quality of service; where necessary, the public health service will recommend changes to improve the quality.

Such difficulties as there are in starting and operating a union health care scheme relate to the preliminary surveys and the initial technical assistance. The surveys should be made by the union itself and should cover, inter alia, such questions as the following: distances and services of the nearest hospitals; nearest doctors; nearest available medical technicians; number and geographical distribution of members interested; types and places of existing services to members; cost of existing services to members; estimate of the amount which members are able and willing to pay for health care; and method and timing of collection of members' contributions at minimum cost. Where the results of such surveys are positive, they should be communicated in full, with a request for technical advice, to the national centre or international trade secretariat.

While many union health care schemes will undoubtedly need free assistance and donated capital, a union should not undertake to provide a health care service if continued outside support will be needed. If that support were to be terminated the service would come to an end, thereby weakening and perhaps even destroying the union.

Child care centres

Background and special needs of members

The establishment of child care centres for the children of working mothers is not of interest to workers in those rural areas where women traditionally do not work outside the home and where there is unlikely to be any early change in that tradition. Nor is there any pressing need for child care centres where the household includes more than two generations, since the oldest generation can look after the youngest. The need does exist, on the other hand, in rural areas where women do work outside the home and in households comprising only two generations, often as the result of migration to a plantation or other large commercial agricultural undertaking.

There was such a need on the part of, for example, some women working in the large agro-industrial complex whose workers are members of the strong union described in the section on "Savings and loan schemes". For these women, there was no older generation in the household who could care for their younger children while they were at work.

Nor is it only rural workers in developing countries who may have special child care needs that their union can service. There is, for example, the case of a developed country with thinly populated rural areas where the fruit and vegetables produced are also canned. Both the agricultural work and the canning work are seasonal and performed largely by migrant workers moving with the season. The canning is often done by women, both local women and the wives of migrant agricultural workers. These women need child care or day care centres for their young children.

Project plans and methods

The first of the two unions referred to above uses 23 per cent of its income and 5 per cent of the income of its co-operative schemes for its educational programmes, and there was money to spare for a child care programme. This union has so far set up two centres, each of them for 300 small children. These centres are equipped with a clinic, a school, dormitories and playrooms, and the children receive food, medical attention and education. The charge to the member using this service is NU1 a month for each child. As the average income of the lowest-paid group in this union is only NU 150 a month, the union is performing an important service by thus catering for the special needs of working mothers.

In the case of the union in a developed country, the base or local unit is small and situated very far away from the national organisation. This local unit made use of a government assistance programme designed to help working mothers in cities. After reading the rules and regulations governing the establishment of free child care centres by local governments qualified to receive funds for that purpose from the national government, the union applied to its local government and at the same time carried on a publicity campaign to enlist the sympathy and support of the women in the area. This support was necessary because most of the agricultural workers, being migrants, were not politically important to the local government. The union also offered that some of its officers should be among the unpaid volunteers forming a board or commission to supervise the centre. The plan was accepted by the local government and approved by the national government.

Observations and conclusions

While the number of rural workers who need a child care service is comparatively small, the service is very important to those who do need it. Its inclusion in this book shows the wide variety of rural workers' needs that can be met by their organisations through special projects. It is also interesting to not how a strong union in a weak national economy met the need for child care solely from its own resources and how a small union of migrants in a strong national economy was able, through the abilities of its leaders, to profit from a government social welfare programme.

What has to be stressed, however, is that there are circumstances in which the need for a rural workers' organisation to provide this type of service itself should not arise. In the plantation industries of some countries, it is the employer's legal responsibility to provide child care services for the children of employees. Where that is the case, the union's task is merely, through representations and pressure, to ensure that the minimum conditions prescribed by law are satisfied and, wherever possible, improved upon.

Legal services

As was noted in the introduction to this book, workers' organisations, including organisations of rural workers, which provide their members with legal services related to their work are employing what is normally one of the traditional methods of furthering and defending their members' interests. However, in the case of rural workers' organisations whose members are peasant farmers, as distinct from wage earners, they are called upon from time to time to provide the membership with so much assistance of a legal and/or administrative nature that it will serve the purposes of this book to treat these activities as special services. (There are, for that matter, also occasions when the legal and/or administrative services provided by organisations of rural wage earners can be regarded, in the context of this book, as special services.)

Background and special needs of members

Four cases of special legal services provided by organisations of rural workers may be usefully considered. The first case concerns the new organisation of sharecroppers, tenants, owner-occupiers of very small plots and landless labourers which was described under Case C. As was noted in the description of that organisation, its main activity was to ensure that the poorest of its members would benefit from any government or other funds for rural development.

The second case concerns a national peasant federation of share-croppers and tenants whose members are seeking better terms with the landlords in a country where not much agrarian reform of any importance is taking place.

The third case concerns a national federation of peasants which was suddenly faced with a decree of a new government granting title of land to the peasants who had been cultivating it over a period of time.

The fourth case concerns a national plantation workers' union, the majority of whose members are stateless, i.e. who are the citizens of no country.

Project plans and methods

In the first case (Case C) the organisation had to engage in a very considerable amount of legal and administrative work on behalf of its peasant members. It had to process large numbers of complicated legal documents and forms required for the purpose of certifying that members' incomes and holdings were small enough to qualify them for participation in various programmes. These legal services, which covered some four-fifths of the membership, will have to be repeated as this new union grows and spreads. Documents and forms also had to be processed in connection with certain government programmes for which only a very small proportion of the membership was eligible. But for these services, few, if any, benefits of the government programmes would reach the members.

The national peasant federation in the second case is over 20 years old and has a large membership in some districts of the country. One of its main activities consists in providing its members with extensive legal and/or administrative services. It appears, indeed, to have the services of more lawyers, both part- and full-time, than any other rural workers' organisation in the world. Although exact information is not available, it seems that most of the services of the lawyers are given free. The federation's legal services cover many types of case but the two main ones are: *(a)* sharecropper or tenant versus landowner cases on an individual basis at the local level; and *(b)* special local cases on behalf of groups of peasants. These cases are taken before the courts, with appeals all the way up to the highest court in the country. When one of the first of the two main types of case is successful, the result is of immediate benefit to one or more members; some aspect of the verbal or written agreement between the member and his landlord is favourably interpreted or altered and results in an increase in income or a decrease in outlay of money or work for the member. In the second of the two main types of case, an attempt is made, sometimes successfully, to obtain rulings by the high courts which are of benefit to all peasants. They constitute, in effect, representations by the union to the judiciary. There was, for example, a decision (constituting a precedent having the force of law) that share-croppers and tenants must be reimbursed by landlords for any permanent improvements made on the land. In another decision it was ruled that rent or shares over a certain percentage of the production were excessive.

The rural workers' organisation in the third case is a ten-year-old national peasant federation in a country where there has been little agrarian reform. The country has a history of sudden changes of government. Following yet another such change, the federation, the national trade union centre and other groups appealed to the new government to introduce wider measures of reform. As earlier appeals to successive new governments had met with little success, the federation and its co-pleaders were unprepared for a decree issued some time later by the new government declaring, in effect, that land belonged to the tiller; this was subject to several qualifications such as a minimum number of years that the land must have been worked by the peasant and a limitation on the amount of land which an individual peasant could claim. It seemed as if the peasants' dream of land of their own had at last come true. A high rate of illiteracy among the peasants (cf. Case C) meant, however, that many, if not most, of them were unable to deal with the legal documents and forms. As the decree prescribed a time-limit for the filing of claims, the federation, whose resources were very limited, had to work night and day to organise a system of processing such as was described under Case C. The federation was able to enlist the free services of some lawyers in advising and training local officers in methods of processing as many valid claims as possible in the shortest possible time.

The very large plantation union in the fourth case has to grapple with a special and very serious problem: the vast majority of its members are not citizens of any country. Their forbears arrived in the country in colonial times to work on the plantations. When the country achieved independence, the descendants of the early plantation workers were not granted citizenship. Accordingly, the union has attempted, through political pressure and representations, to obtain citizenship for as many of its members as possible. Another of the union's main activities consists in providing special legal services in connection with the repatriation of members willing and eligible to go back to the country of their ancestors.

Observations and conclusions

Each of the last three examples is no doubt a special case; but many of the interests of rural workers, especially in developing countries or in developing regions of developed countries, are special cases reflecting social, political, historical, cultural and economic differences between regions and peoples. The strength of the rural workers' trade union movement—which can be much reinforced by special services—lies in its ability to adapt itself to special situations by finding effective methods of furthering and defending all the interests of the membership.

The second of the four cases illustrates, furthermore, the need for all peasant unions to be at least aware of what is involved in the provision of legal and administrative services and to find lawyers who would be ready and able to help in the establishment of such services when they are required.

Part III

Planning and operating special services

Planning and operating special services

The concept

Why and how does a rural workers' organisation become involved in special servicing activities? A rural workers' union turns to these activities because it has not been able to meet one or more of the needs of its members by means of the traditional union methods of defending and furthering the interests of members: negotiations, pressure-group activities and representation.

A union of agricultural wage earners may be unable to negotiate wage increases which keep up with or exceed rises in the cost of living, or to obtain by representation government action to control prices of first-necessity items. As we have seen, in this situation the union may turn to consumer activities.

A peasant federation has a list of specific demands reflecting the membership's concept of needed agrarian reform. If the federation has not been able to obtain a significant reform programme from government through pressure-group activities and representation, it may turn to special services as a means of tackling some of the outstanding needs of members, while continuing the pressure for reform.

Examples have been noted of rural unions providing special services in order to meet the particular needs of only a segment of the membership, such as tube-wells for peasants (Case C) and child care centre schemes for working mothers (see section on "Child care centres" above).

Instances where rural unions have taken the initiative in identifying needs to be met by special services have been noted—for example, the organisation of plantation workers considered under Case A attacked the problem of unemployment among its members by developing industries to create new jobs.

Survey stage

To decide whether or not a need of members can and should be met by a special service requires a considerable amount of detailed information collection. Usually, a rural workers' organisation in a developing country is faced with several outstanding needs of members, and gains some idea of the members' views on which need has the highest priority. The organisation must first obtain a great deal of qualitative and quantitative information on the exact nature of the need, in order that the service that may be developed does in fact meet the need that exists. Following this, more information and analysis are necessary to determine once again if all or part of the need can be satisfied through negotiation and/or representation or whether, as seen in some examples, the need can be met by a combination of traditional and special services.

Detailed information must also be collected to determine what resources (personnel, technical knowledge and experience, facilities, finances) will be required to initiate the special service under consideration. A similar exercise is needed to determine what resources are available within the organisation and what assistance may be sought from its officers and officials and its members. If these surveys indicate that the resources available fall short of what is needed to start the service, information must be sought regarding possible sources from which the specific missing resources might be obtained.

In addition, and separately, the cost of operating the special service must be analysed. If capital goods such as the medical vans in the example considered under Case D are involved, any estimate of the cost of operating the service must include an allowance for the creation of a reserve fund to replace those capital goods in the future. Again, information must be obtained to determine whether sufficient resources are available to meet the costs of operating the service. As noted in several examples, special payments by members receiving a special service are sometimes necessary to meet the costs of operating some services, and detailed information is needed on the ability and willingness of members to make such payments.

Detailed information collection and analysis does not guarantee the success of a special service; but the lack of it greatly increases the chances of failure.

Planning stage

With the information obtained from the various surveys, the workers' organisation can take some preliminary decisions as to whether or not a special service can and should be used to meet a particular need of members. Obviously, if the initial costs of the service are beyond the resources of the union or beyond the amount that the union believes it might be able to obtain through the participation of others, there is no point in continuing. Moreover, if the costs of operating the service are beyond the ability of receiving members to pay—if this is necessary—an organisation can go no further with this particular special servicing idea.

Assuming, however, that all the resources necessary to start the service and to operate it are available or can be obtained, the organisation must next put a proposed plan of action on paper. A written plan serves as a basis for examination, criticism, suggestions, refinements and amendments by the officers and officials of the union; it also serves as a basis for examination by interested technical groups who may be able to give advice and suggestions, by other organisations participating in the service, if that is the situation, and finally (and most important) by the members themselves, for their ideas and approval.

The plan should contain all relevant and necessary information collected during the earlier surveys. There are many ways to organise a written plan; perhaps the simplest way is on the basis of "why, who, when, where and how".

■ *Why?* This section should define clearly and in detail the need of members to be met by the proposed special service; state why the need cannot be met by the traditional methods of a workers' organisation; and indicate how any facts and figures given were obtained.

■ *Who?* This section should list in detail the groups of members for whom the service will be provided; how many members are involved, and in which areas; and all the evidence obtained (and how obtained) in support of the belief that these members want and are prepared to use and support the service.

■ *When?* This section should establish any appropriate time estimates for the various stages of the plan; when and for how long an education or information programme needs to be organised among the members concerning the service to be introduced; the timing of preparations for any facilities required; and the proposed starting dates of the service, by area.

■ *Where?* This section should give the location of any service facilities and the information on which the decision regarding that location was based.

■ *How?* This section makes up a very large part of any written plan. It should indicate in detail how the service is to be administered and how finances are to be handled. To avoid repetition, general and financial administration are discussed in the next section, but these matters would be included here in the plan.

Operations

General and financial administration are important to the development and operation of a rural workers' organisation, and the same is true for any special service that may be undertaken. The same principles and practices of good administration as are applicable to the development and operation of a peasant federation or a rural wage earners' organisation apply also to the development and operation of a marketing scheme, a consumer activity, a technical agrarian service or any other special service. Rural workers' leaders who feel that their organisation's administrative and financial procedures and practices are not yet perfectly sound should not attempt to introduce a special service but should first put their union's house in order.

Organisational structure

One of the first and most important administrative decisions to be taken concerns the organisational structure or form of the special service to be provided. The structure should be kept as simple as possible. If some of the case examples of special services observed earlier are re-examined, it will be seen how the organisational forms chosen are adapted to meet the degree of complexity and the administrative situations encountered.

Perhaps the simplest type of situation is offered by the example of the child care centre, where the union in effect took over an existing government social welfare programme; if the union officers and officials serving as part of a volunteer executive board for the programme are left out of account, it emerges that in fact the union got another organisation to provide the service, but with policy determined by the union itself.

Community development services are somewhat similar, in that officers at the base level are the main activists in this type of service, with the peasant federation furnishing only advice and technical expertise as and if required.

Many types of educational service, such as workers' education, health, nutrition, family planning or literacy training, require the acquisition of materials, facilities and teachers or the training of union officers as teachers; but usually the service can be administered within the union structure by increasing the work and responsibilities of officials and/or officers. (This would not be true if all the types of education programme cited were carried on simultaneously—an education section would then be required within the union.)

A technical agrarian service is another activity that usually does not require new organisational structures: the duties and responsibilities of the field representative are enlarged to include this special service, and union officials see to it that he is given appropriate training and does in fact provide this service to members.

Legal services are a special case in that either they may be handled within the existing union operation and administration or, in special situations, a separate structure may be needed. In the example offered by Case C, the volume of legal and administrative servicing became extremely large and much of the work was done by volunteer unemployed literate youths. Had these youngsters not been available and willing, paid assistance would have been necessary and significant additional costs would have been incurred. Without the young volunteers, this activity would have required a separate unit within the union, with additional administrative and financial procedures.

Case C also provides another illustration of the principle of keeping the organisational structure, and hence the administration, of a special service as simple as possible. As noted, this peasant union is only one year old; at present it operates in only one area, but it offers a wide range of special services. So far it has been able to accomplish everything within the present union structure and its administrative and financial practices and procedures; but as the services grow and as the union begins to operate in other areas, it will no longer be possible for it to manage several services with the help of only its officers and officials and with financial resources derived solely from dues. In particular, new organisational forms will be required to manage purchasing and marketing activities if the union is to provide the best possible service for its members.

This leads to the examples of Cases A and B. The national federation of peasant farmers described under Case B established four different enterprises to provide purchasing and marketing services for its members. These were formed and registered as enterprises or companies under the laws of the country. The scope of these special services, expressed in terms of the personnel needed to operate them on a national level and the capital investment needed to start them, clearly called for a separate organisational structure. One way to set about this is to form a co-operative, which provides an excellent organisational, administrative and financial structure for the two special services in question; the alternative, where the national legislation does not permit any limitation on the membership in co-operatives, is to establish enterprises or companies.

Similarly, to create new jobs for unemployed members, the organisation of plantation workers described under Case A is establishing new industries in plantation areas and forming enterprises or companies so as to provide the simplest organisational structure to manage the complex administration and finances of this special service; and it is often doing so on a joint venture basis with government and/or private companies. This brings in outside administrative skills and experience as well as additional investment.

The organisation of seasonal agricultural wage earners described under Case D, which has migrant members working in an extremely isolated and unhealthy area devoid of all social welfare facilities, was formed by the rural workers with the specific goal of starting special services requiring outside technical personnel and special financing. This union established a "welfare department" within the union administrative structure, with a separate financial operation paid for by special welfare dues from participating members. The head of the welfare department is appointed by and serves under the union's executive committee. The first head of this department is a former member of a plantation union in another part of the country: he has had training in administration and accounting and has worked in a plantation office and for a credit union. This "department system" is an excellent and simple way of organising and controlling some of the larger or more complex special services which do not require the co-operative or enterprise type of organisational structure.

The best example of the use of the department system is that of the strong enterprise union of 12,000 members referred to under "Housing schemes" and elsewhere. This union, under a special services section within the union structure, has six departments (one for each of its six special services), thereby maintaining simplicity and control over a wide variety of activities.

General administration

To obtain maximum results, the resources available for operating a special service—personnel and finances—must be used as efficiently and effectively as possible. This requires the development of centralised administration, control and finances.

Personnel

All staff working on a special service, including technicians who have to be hired from outside the membership, need to be made and kept "trade union conscious", in the sense of understanding what trade unionism is, of understanding that the special service exists because there is a union and not vice versa, and that they, the staff, are at the service of and paid by the members. Some special services are of a nature such that some voluntary help by members can be used at times; where applicable, this should be encouraged and developed. All opportunities to send staff engaged on special services to related training programmes should be utilised. Special services can and are being used to extend and maintain membership in the union, and all officers and officials engaged in such services should be trained, under union rules and practices, to enrol new members and to collect dues from current members. Those in charge of administering a service must continually review the operation and provide remedies or education where administrative problems exist.

Control and collaborators

A workers' organisation exists to further and defend the interests of members as defined by the members, and elected union leaders cannot delegate this responsibility to any organisation or person outside the union. In those special services requiring an outside collaborator on a continuing basis (such as a vocational training programme operated jointly by a union and a vocational training institute), the plan of and any agreement relating to the special service should clearly state policies and objectives and also that these can be changed only with the approval of the union.

Control and delegation of authority

Those special services which are performed by union officers or officials (for instance, in the case where technical agrarian services are added to the duties and responsibilities of field representatives) will follow the current union policies and practices of delegation and control. In the more complex situations the executive committee of the rural workers' organisation establishes policies regarding the service; officials of the union implement these policies; and the staff of a special service operate it in conformity with the established policies. For example, the head of the welfare services department of the organisation of seasonal agricultural wage earners considered under Case D administers the medical scheme within the policies established by the organisation's executive committee, and the operation of this service is carried out by the chief medical technician and his assistants under the administrative (not technical) procedures and practices established by the department head. Where enterprises or companies are formed, the union's executive committee decides or influences policy, and the administration and operation are left to technical and management personnel. Rural workers' organisations providing special services should periodically review the amount of authority delegated to those responsible for operating the services to see that sufficient authority is being delegated to operate the service effectively and efficiently; but that at the same time it is not so much that policy is, in effect, being changed by staff.

Two-way communications

All personnel engaged on special services should be instructed in providing two-way communications: advising a designated union official of the criticisms and praise of members on specific aspects of the service; and advising members of union actions and plans in relation to the service as these are provided to the staff by the designated official. Only with this exchange of information between those receiving the service and those establishing policies and practices can the service develop and meet the real needs of members.

Financial administration

As with general administration, financial administration should be kept as simple as possible. There are, however, procedures and practices which have long been established and proven in use by workers' organisations around the world. As already observed, a rural workers' organisation without a well functioning system of financial administration should rectify this situation before contemplating the establishment of a special service. The national centre or an international trade secretariat can help in this matter if requested.

Assuming that a rural workers' organisation itself has a simple but effective system of procedures and practices for recording and controlling all moneys received and all moneys paid out and a system for having the records and controls verified by auditors, it should have no problems in applying these systems to any special service.

Any special service operated and administered within the regular organisational structure of the union and requiring no separate finance from members will need no new or separate book-keeping or other financial procedures. In these simpler cases a federation or union should periodically monitor the number of man-hours being devoted by staff to the special service and also the amount of cash expenditure. If one or both of these become large, the executive committee might have to consider raising dues, if the service is wanted and used by all members; or establishing fees to be paid by receiving members, if the service is needed and used by only one group of the membership.

Two examples of fee systems have been observed: a flat rate of NUs based on the costs in man-hours involved in applications for grants or loans; or a percentage (usually 2 per cent) of any loans received through the processing of the application by the federation. The principle involved here is important—when a special service becomes a burden on a union's organisational structure and/or finances, a separate structure and/or funding are required.

The enterprises or companies established by the organisation described under Case A to combat unemployment and by the federation described under Case B to provide purchasing and marketing services for members are examples of situations where good administration (and the law) require that a separate financial administration should exist. The executive committees of these rural workers' organisations receive copies of the financial statements of these enterprises and control or influence their policies and decisions relating to financial administration, usually as members of the enterprise's board of directors.

The medical scheme operated under the welfare department of the organisation considered under Case D, while directly and completely under the control of the executive committee of the union, does require double book-keeping and control because of the double system of dues. All members pay NU 2 a month as union dues, and those members receiving the service provided under the union medical scheme pay an additional NU 2 a month to the union welfare fund, this to be used only for the special service. The practices and procedures for recording moneys received and moneys paid out under the union general fund and under the union welfare fund are identical, but there is a separate set of books for each fund. There is one exception—the executive committee can authorise payments from the union welfare fund only for expenses related to the special service. Since there are separate funds, there are two financial statements; but both go to, and are under the control of, the union executive committee.

The enterprise union which uses the department system of structured organisation, with sections for each of six different special services, submits a variety of financial reports to the executive committee; the financial procedures and practices are, however, the same as for other organisations. Some sections have their own set of books—the savings and loan scheme needs this for reasons of good administration as well as to meet legal requirements. But the control of moneys received (where applicable) and of moneys spent by these special services is either directly under the executive committee of the union (as in most cases) or, for those activities such as the savings and loan scheme where the law requires it, under the control of a board of directors composed of union members and officers; again, copies of financial statements are sent to the union executive committee.

Whether a rural workers' organisation is operating a single and relatively simple special service or a variety of complex services some of which require the separate recording and control of income and out-goings, the same basic principles, practices and procedures that underlie the good financial administration of the rural workers' organisation itself can and should be applied to special services. It cannot be repeated too often that, if the rural workers' organisation does not already have good financial administration, higher priority must be given to acquiring a satisfactory system than to any special service.

Conclusion

It is as well to end this book with a repetition of one of the points made in the early pages: special services, whether undertaken by rural or by urban workers' organisations, are only a means—they are not an end. The end, for a workers' organisation, is always, and simply, to further and defend the interests of its members. If the needs of the members can be satisfactorily furthered or defended by traditional trade union methods, the organisation has no need to develop special services.

But if members have a need that is not being met by the traditional methods of negotiation, pressure-group activities or representation, the organisation concerned has to consider whether that need can be met by the provision of a special service.

In these pages we have looked at the range of such services as might be undertaken by a single organisation, and we have looked at services by category, to show how the same type of service might be approached in different circumstances. But it is also important to appreciate that all the examples have one thing in common: that before the special service could be undertaken, there had first to be a rural workers' organisation to undertake it.

In other words, whilst a special service may, as we have seen, be provided to build and strengthen the organisation, and whilst it can often be critical in maintaining the strength and effectiveness of the organisation, the service is only one part of the means to fulfil the end purpose for which the members originally formed and joined the organisation.

Provided that these points are always kept firmly in mind, the next most important stage is that covered in Part III—identifying the needs which are not being met by traditional methods and which might be met by a special service, selecting the service or services that meet the optimum combination of priority of need and practicability of application and operation, planning their introduction and ensuring their adequate administration and financial control.

All those stages are marked by often delicate decisions and place considerable responsibility on the leaders of the organisation—a responsibility which they can effectively shoulder only if all their plans and proposals are fully discussed with, and have adequate support from, the members (which again reminds us that there first has to be an organisation, and that the planned service is the servant and not the master of the organisation—it is a means to an end).

Within this context the special service can be a major factor in ensuring the effectiveness with which an organisation furthers and defends the interests of its members, not only in the sphere of the service itself, but also in a wider context. It is hoped that the issues and examples which have been reviewed in these pages will provide a practical contribution to that end; and thus to the ultimate objective of achieving a situation where rural workers everywhere have strong and independent organisations of their own choosing, capable of ensuring their ability to participate effectively in the processes of social and economic development—both for themselves as individuals and for their countries.

Appendix

ILO Convention concerning Organisations of Rural Workers and Their Role in Economic and Social Development, 1975 (No. 141)[1]

The General Conference of the International Labour Organisation,

Having been convened at Geneva by the Governing Body of the International Labour Office, and having met in its Sixtieth Session on 4 June 1975, and

Recognising that the importance of rural workers in the world makes it urgent to associate them with economic and social development action if their conditions of work and life are to be permanently and effectively improved, and

Noting that in many countries of the world and particularly in developing countries there is massive under-utilisation of land and labour and that this makes it imperative for rural workers to be given every encouragement to develop free and viable organisations capable of protecting and furthering the interests of their members and ensuring their effective contribution to economic and social development, and

Considering that such organisations can and should contribute to the alleviation of the persistent scarcity of food products in various regions of the world, and

Recognising that land reform is in many developing countries an essential factor in the improvement of the conditions of work and life of rural workers and that organisations of such workers should accordingly co-operate and participate actively in the implementation of such reform, and

Recalling the terms of existing international labour Conventions and Recommendations—in particular the Right of Association (Agriculture) Convention, 1921, the Freedom of Association and Protection of the Right to Organise Convention, 1948, and the Right to Organise and Collective Bargaining Convention, 1949—which affirm the right of all workers, including rural workers, to establish free and independent organisations, and the provisions of numerous international labour Conventions and Recommendations applicable to rural workers which call for the participation, inter alia, of workers' organisations in their implementation, and

---

[1] Preamble and excerpts from substantive provisions.

Noting the joint concern of the United Nations and the specialised agencies, in particular the International Labour Organisation and the Food and Agriculture Organisation of the United Nations, with land reform and rural development, and

Noting that the following standards have been framed in co-operation with the Food and Agriculture Organisation of the United Nations and that, with a view to avoiding duplication, there will be continuing co-operation with that Organisation and with the United Nations in promoting and securing the application of these standards, and

Having decided upon the adoption of certain proposals with regard to organisations of rural workers and their role in economic and social development, which is the fourth item on the agenda of the session, and

Having determined that these proposals shall take the form of an international Convention,

adopts this twenty-third day of June of the year one thousand nine hundred and seventy-five the following Convention, which may be cited as the Rural Workers' Organisations Convention, 1975:

Article 1

This Convention applies to all types of organisations of rural workers, including organisations not restricted to but representative of rural workers.

Article 2

1. For the purposes of this Convention, the term "rural workers" means any person engaged in agriculture, handicrafts or a related occupation in a rural area, whether as a wage earner or, subject to the provisions of paragraph 2 of this Article, as a self-employed person such as a tenant, sharecropper or small owner-occupier.

2. This Convention applies only to those tenants, sharecroppers or small owner-occupiers who derive their main income from agriculture, who work the land themselves, with the help only of their family or with the help of occasional outside labour and who do not—

(a) permanently employ workers; or

(b) employ a substantial number of seasonal workers; or

(c) have any land cultivated by sharecroppers or tenants.

Article 3

1. All categories of rural workers, whether they are wage earners or self-employed, shall have the right to establish and, subject only to the rules of the organisation concerned, to join organisations of their own choosing without previous authorisation.

2. The principles of freedom of association shall be fully respected; rural workers' organisations shall be independent and voluntary in character and shall remain free from all interference, coercion or repression.

3. The acquisition of legal personality by organisations of rural workers shall not be made subject to conditions of such a character as to restrict the application of the provisions of the preceding paragraphs of this Article.

4. In exercising the rights provided for in this Article rural workers and their respective organisations, like other persons or organised collectivities, shall respect the law of the land.

5. The law of the land shall not be such as to impair, nor shall it to be so applied as to impair, the guarantees provided for in this Article.

Article 4

It shall be an objective of national policy concerning rural development to facilitate the establishment and growth, on a voluntary basis, of strong and independent organisations of rural workers as an effective means of ensuring the participation of rural workers, without discrimination as defined in the Discrimination (Employment and Occupation) Convention, 1958, in economic and social development and in the benefits resulting therefrom.

Article 5

1. In order to enable organisations of rural workers to play their role in economic and social development, each Member which ratifies this Convention shall adopt and carry out a policy of active encouragement to these organisations, particularly with a view to eliminating obstacles to their establishment, their growth and the pursuit of their lawful activities, as well as such legislative and administrative discrimination against rural workers' organisations and their members as may exist.

2. Each Member which ratifies this Convention shall ensure that national laws or regulations do not, given the special circumstances of the rural sector, inhibit the establishment and growth of rural workers' organisations.

Article 6

Steps shall be taken to promote the widest possible understanding of the need to further the development of rural workers' organisations and of the contribution they can make to improving employment opportunities and general conditions of work and life in rural areas as well as to increasing the national income and achieving a better distribution thereof.

. . . .